Contents

D0524737

A note on nutrition: All recipes in this cookbook were developed and tested in The Pampered Chef Test Kitchens by professional home economists. At the end of each recipe, we list calories, total fat, sodium and dietary fiber. Nutritional content of these recipes is based on food composition data in The Pampered Chef database. Variations in ingredients, products and measurements may result in approximate values. Each analysis is based on ingredients initially listed and does not include optional ingredients, garnishes, fat used to grease pans or serving suggestions, unless noted. Recipes requiring milk are based on 2 percent reduced-fat milk. Recipes requiring ground beef are analyzed based on 90 percent lean ground beef.

4

········· *"Simply Sensational!"* ·········

That was the response to our first **Stoneware Sensations** cookbook. Now **More Stoneware Sensations** is here highlighting all the Stoneware including our newest additions in our Family Heritage® Collection. It brings you over sixty exclusive recipes along with beautiful color photographs. The results are – well – simply sensational!

Each easy and convenient recipe in **More Stoneware Sensations** will give you delicious and dramatic results. From the delectable *Chocolate Satin Mint Cake* featured on our cover to traditional recipes with a special twist like our *All-American Cheeseburger Ring*, this cookbook contains the recipes, tips and techniques that you'll turn to time and time again.

So gather your family and friends together and serve them something special. Believe me, they'll think you're simply sensational!

Warm regards,

Doris Christopher
Founder and President
The Pampered Chef, Ltd.

The Pampered Chef is the premier direct-seller of high-quality kitchen tools sold through in-home Kitchen Shows presented by Kitchen Consultants across the U.S. and Canada. At Kitchen Shows, guests enjoy product and recipe demonstrations, learn about quick and easy food preparation ideas, and have lots of fun!

Founded in 1980 by educator and home economist Doris Christopher, and headquartered in Addison, Illinois, The Pampered Chef is committed to enhancing family life by providing quality kitchen products supported by service and information.

Cover Recipe: Chocolate Satin Mint Cake p. 84

Clockwise from bottom front: Loaf Pan (featuring *Spiced Carrot-Zucchini Bread*, p. 38), Bar Pan, Fluted Pan, Rectangular Lid/Bowl, 9" x 13" Baker (featuring *Lasagna Primavera*, p. 58), Baking Bowl, 9" Square Baker, 15" Round Baking Stone with Oven-To-Table Rack (featuring *Fruit-Topped Triple Chocolate Pizza*, p. 75), 12" x 15" Rectangle Baking Stone (featuring *Cranberry Macadamia Oat Cookies*, p. 82). Center: 8" Mini-Baker and Deep Dish Baker (featuring *BBQ Chicken Twister*, p. 65).

Awesome Appetizers

For casual gatherings or festive parties, we bring you more tasty appetizers. You'll find Stoneware Bowls and Bakers are ideal for keeping cheesy fondues and spreads warm while serving. On our flat Baking Stones, savory-filled pastries and tortilla treats bake up crisp and golden. Choose your favorite stoneware recipes, then get the party rolling.

Antipasto Bread

The zesty-flavored ingredients of a traditional Italian antipasto platter come alive in this savory bread ring. Serve it for an appetizer or alongside soup, salad or pasta.

1   jar (6½ ounces) marinated artichoke hearts, drained
⅓   cup sliced deli hard salami, chopped
⅓   cup red bell pepper, chopped
½   cup pitted ripe olives, sliced
2   garlic cloves, pressed
¼   cup butter or margarine, melted
4   ounces fresh Parmesan cheese, grated (about 1 cup)
2   packages (11.3 ounces each) refrigerated dinner rolls

Preheat oven to 375°F. Spray **Stoneware Fluted Pan** with nonstick cooking spray. Place artichokes on paper towels; pat dry. Chop artichokes, salami and bell pepper using **Food Chopper**; place in **1-Qt. Batter Bowl**. Slice olives using **Egg Slicer Plus®** Add olives and garlic pressed with **Garlic Press** to Batter Bowl; mix lightly and set aside. Melt butter in **Covered Micro-Cooker®** on HIGH 30 seconds. Using **Deluxe Cheese Grater**, grate Parmesan cheese into **Classic 2-Qt. Batter Bowl**. Separate dinner rolls and cut each into quarters using **Kitchen Shears**. Dip 16 dough pieces in melted butter, then roll in cheese. Arrange evenly in pan. Sprinkle with ½ cup of the artichoke mixture. Repeat twice. Dip remaining 16 dough pieces in melted butter, roll in cheese and arrange over last layer of artichoke mixture. Sprinkle with any remaining cheese. Bake 27-30 minutes or until deep golden brown. Cool 5 minutes on **Nonstick Cooling Rack**. Loosen edges of bread from side and center of pan with **Citrus Peeler**. Carefully invert onto Cooling Rack to remove bread. Cool slightly. Slice with **Serrated Bread Knife**.

Yield: 16 servings

Nutrients per serving: Calories 190, Fat 9 g, Sodium 280 mg, Dietary Fiber 2 g

COOK'S TIP

■ *The easiest (and neatest) way to coat dough pieces in cheese is to use one hand for dipping dough pieces in melted butter and the other hand for rolling pieces in the cheese.*

TOOL TIP

■ *There's no need to peel your garlic cloves before pressing when using our **Garlic Press**. When cloves are pressed, the garlic flesh gets forced through the holes, while the papery skin stays in the hopper.*

Roasted Garlic Spread

Two heads of garlic in one recipe may seem like a lot, but roasted fresh garlic is mild, slightly nutty and truly delicious. Enjoy its distinctive flavor in this Mediterranean-style appetizer.

2	whole heads garlic, unpeeled
3	plum tomatoes, each cut into 4 wedges
1	tablespoon olive oil
1	container (8 ounces) chive & onion soft cream cheese
1/4	teaspoon dried oregano leaves
1/4	teaspoon salt

Preheat oven to 425°F. Slice off top quarter of each garlic head to expose garlic cloves. (Do not separate cloves.) Place in center of **8" Mini-Baker**; surround with tomato wedges. Drizzle oil over garlic and tomatoes. Cover with **Mini-Baking Bowl**. Bake 40-45 minutes or until garlic is soft and golden brown; cool completely. Gently squeeze garlic heads from root ends to remove roasted garlic cloves from papery skins; place in **1-Qt. Batter Bowl**. Chop tomatoes using **Food Chopper**; transfer to Batter Bowl using **Kitchen Scraper**. Add cream cheese, oregano and salt; mix well. Chill until ready to serve. Serve with *Baked Pita Chips*.

Yield: 1 1/2 cups (12 servings)

Nutrients per serving (2 tablespoons spread): Calories 90, Fat 7 g, Sodium 115 mg, Dietary Fiber 0 g

Baked Pita Chips

3	whole pita bread rounds

Preheat oven to 400°F. Using **Pizza Cutter**, cut each pita bread round horizontally in half. Cut each half into 8 triangles. Arrange pita triangles in single layer on flat **Baking Stone**. Bake 8-10 minutes or until lightly browned and crisp.

Yield: 48 chips (12 servings)

Nutrients per serving (4 chips per serving): Calories 40, Fat 0 g, Sodium 80 mg, Dietary Fiber 0 g

COOK'S TIP

- *You can use roasted garlic in many delicious ways. Simply prepare garlic as directed above (omitting tomatoes), then use to spread on French bread, mix in creamy salad dressing, toss with hot cooked pasta or add to mashed potatoes.*

Cheesy Cheddar Fondue

Natural cheddar cheese and canned cheese soup are oven melted for the creamiest, cheesiest dipping sauce ever. The Mini-Baking Bowl keeps the fondue warm while serving.

8	ounces mild cheddar cheese, shredded (2 cups)
2	tablespoons all-purpose flour
1	can (10¾ ounces) condensed cheddar cheese soup
¾	cup non-alcoholic beer or milk
1	loaf (8 ounces) rye bread, cut into 1-inch cubes

Preheat oven to 350°F. Using **Deluxe Cheese Grater**, shred cheese into **Mini-Baking Bowl**. Add flour; toss. Stir in soup and non-alcoholic beer. Bake 30 minutes or until cheese is melted and smooth when stirred. Using **Serrated Bread Knife**, cut rye bread into 1-inch cubes. Use **Bamboo Tongs**, fondue forks or wooden skewers to dip bread cubes into fondue.

Yield: 8 servings (2⅔ cups fondue)

Nutrients per serving (approximately ⅓ cup fondue and ⅛ of bread): Calories 210, Fat 9 g, Sodium 710 mg, Dietary Fiber 2 g

COOK'S TIPS

- *To prepare fondue in microwave oven, combine fondue ingredients in **Mini-Baking Bowl** as directed. Microwave on HIGH 2 minutes. Stir; continue microwaving 2-3 minutes, stirring every minute, until cheese is melted and smooth. If fondue cools while serving, return to microwave oven and microwave on HIGH 1-2 minutes, stirring every minute, until mixture is heated.*

- *In addition to using rye bread cubes for dipping, try sourdough or French bread cubes; soft breadsticks; apple or pear wedges; chicken, turkey or ham chunks; bell pepper strips; or partially cooked vegetables such as small red potatoes, cut in half, broccoli flowerets or cauliflowerets.*

TOOL TIP

- *When prepared in the conventional oven, Cheesy Cheddar Fondue stays warm for up to 30 minutes due to the heat retention of the stoneware **Mini-Baking Bowl**.*

Appetizers

Spinach Diamond Puffs

A savory spinach filling is wrapped in a square of
tender puff pastry for an elegant party nibble.

1 package (10 ounces) frozen
  chopped spinach, thawed and
  drained
1/2 cup carrots, finely chopped
1 tablespoon onion, finely chopped
1/2 cup mayonnaise
1/4 teaspoon ground nutmeg
1/4 teaspoon salt
4 ounces Swiss cheese, shredded
  (1 cup)
1 package (17.25 ounces) frozen
  puff pastry sheets, thawed
1 egg, lightly beaten
1 tablespoon water

Preheat oven to 425°F. Cover **12" x 15" Rectangle Baking Stone** with **Parchment Paper**. Place drained spinach on paper towels and press to remove excess moisture. Chop carrots and onion using **Food Chopper**. Place spinach, carrots, onion, mayonnaise and seasonings in **Classic 2-Qt. Batter Bowl**. Shred cheese into Batter Bowl using **Deluxe Cheese Grater**; mix well. Lightly sprinkle flat side of **18" x 12" Grooved Cutting Board** with flour. Using floured **Dough and Pizza Roller**, roll one pastry sheet into a 12-inch square. (Wrap second pastry sheet in plastic wrap and refrigerate until ready to use.) Cut rolled pastry into sixteen 3-inch squares using **Pizza Cutter**. (Do not separate squares.) Using small **Stainless Steel Scoop**, place a scant scoop spinach mixture in center of each square. Flatten slightly with back of scoop. Combine egg and water. Using **Pastry Brush**, brush egg mixture over cut lines in pastry and around outside edge of large square. For each appetizer, bring two opposite corners of each square up over filling, pinch together firmly and twist. Place on Baking Stone. Brush appetizers with egg mixture. Bake 17-18 minutes or until golden brown. Remove to serving platter using **Mini-Serving Spatula**. Repeat with remaining pastry sheet and spinach mixture. Serve warm.

Yield: 32 appetizers

Nutrients per serving (2 appetizers): Calories 240, Fat 16 g,
Sodium 210 mg, Dietary Fiber 3 g

COOK'S TIP

- The spinach mixture can be made ahead of time and refrigerated, but assemble and bake the puffs just before serving.

Cheddar Potato Puffs

For party snacks with down-home flavor, try these mashed potatoes with garlic, cheese and bacon. They're scooped into bite-size balls and baked in a crunchy coating.

4   ounces sharp cheddar cheese,
       shredded (1 cup)
4   slices bacon, crisply cooked and
       chopped
2   tablespoons green onions with
       tops, finely chopped
1   garlic clove, pressed
2   cups instant mashed potato flakes
1½   cups milk
¼   cup mayonnaise
1   egg, lightly beaten
¼   teaspoon salt
1½   cups corn flake cereal

Preheat oven to 375°F. Using **Deluxe Cheese Grater**, shred cheese into **Classic 2-Qt. Batter Bowl**. Chop bacon and green onions using **Food Chopper**; add to Batter Bowl. Press garlic into cheese mixture using **Garlic Press**. Add potato flakes, milk, mayonnaise, egg and salt; mix well. Crush cereal in large, resealable plastic bag using **Dough and Pizza Roller**. Shape potato mixture into balls using small **Stainless Steel Scoop**. Place several potato balls in plastic bag; shake bag to coat. Remove potato balls and arrange on **15" Round Baking Stone**. Repeat with remaining potato balls. Bake 20 minutes. Serve warm.

Yield: 48 potato puffs

Nutrients per serving (2 potato puffs): Calories 130, Fat 4 g, Sodium 150 mg, Dietary Fiber 1 g

COOK'S TIP

■ *Potato puffs can be made up to two days in advance. Prepare as directed except for baking. Place in single layer in covered container; refrigerate. When ready to serve, arrange on* **15" Round Baking Stone** *and bake as directed.*

California Appetizer Pizza

If you like avocados, you'll love this refreshing pizza topped with creamy guacamole, delicate seafood and fresh, ripe tomatoes.

1 package (8 ounces) refrigerated crescent rolls
2 ripe avocados, peeled and mashed (about 1 cup)
2 tablespoons onion, finely chopped
1 lemon
1/4 cup sour cream
1/2 teaspoon salt
4 ounces Monterey Jack cheese, shredded (1 cup)
4 ounces flake- or leg-style imitation crabmeat, chopped
2 plum tomatoes, seeded and chopped
2 tablespoons fresh cilantro or parsley, snipped

Preheat oven to 350°F. Unroll crescent dough; separate into 8 triangles. On **13" Round Baking Stone**, arrange triangles in a circle with points in the center and wide ends toward the outside. Using lightly floured **Dough and Pizza Roller**, roll out dough to a 12-inch circle, pressing seams together to seal. Bake 12-15 minutes or until light golden brown. Remove from oven. Cool completely. In **Classic 2-Qt. Batter Bowl**, mash avocados using **Nylon Masher**. Finely chop onion using **Food Chopper**. Juice lemon to measure 2 teaspoons lemon juice using **Lemon Aid**. Add sour cream, onion, lemon juice and salt to avocado; mix well. Spread mixture evenly over crust using **Skinny Scraper**. Using **Deluxe Cheese Grater**, shred cheese evenly over avocado mixture. Coarsely chop crabmeat using Food Chopper. Sprinkle crabmeat and tomatoes over cheese. Snip cilantro using **Kitchen Shears**; sprinkle over top. Cut into squares with **Pizza Cutter**; serve using **Mini-Serving Spatula**.

Yield: 10 servings

Nutrients per serving: Calories 210, Fat 16 g, Sodium 530 mg, Dietary Fiber 2 g

COOK'S TIP

■ *Many supermarket avocados are hard and unripe. To ripen, place in a paper bag at room temperature for several days. Avocados are ready to use when they yield to gentle pressure. To prepare an avocado, cut in half lengthwise to the pit, then gently twist the halves in opposite directions to pull apart. Firmly press knife blade into the pit and twist knife to pull out pit. Scoop flesh out of skin with a spoon.*

TOOL TIP

■ *A quick squeeze of fresh lemon juice, needed to keep the mashed avocados from turning brown, is always on hand when you use the **Lemon Aid**. Insert the Lemon Aid, with its unique capped spout, into fresh lemons or limes then place fruit in the handy storage container for refrigeration. Be ready with fresh juice for recipes or enjoy a splash of citrus on fruits or in beverages.*

Blue Cheese Spread

*Enjoy this warm cheese spread with fresh apple and
pear wedges or Toasted Canapé Bread Slices.*

2   packages (8 ounces each) cream
     cheese, softened
1/2 cup (2 ounces) crumbled blue
     cheese
1/3 cup celery, finely chopped
1   tablespoon onion, finely chopped
1   teaspoon lemon juice
1/2 teaspoon Worcestershire sauce
     Dash ground red pepper
1/3 cup walnuts, chopped
1   tablespoon fresh parsley, snipped

Preheat oven to 325°F. In **Classic 2-Qt. Batter Bowl**, mix cream cheese and blue cheese until well blended. Finely chop celery and onion using **Food Chopper**; add to Batter Bowl. Add lemon juice, Worcestershire sauce and ground red pepper to cream cheese mixture; mix well. Spread evenly in **8" Mini-Baker**. Chop walnuts using Food Chopper; sprinkle over cream cheese mixture. Bake 25-30 minutes or until thoroughly heated. Snip parsley with **Kitchen Shears**; sprinkle over spread. Serve warm with apples or pears cut with **Apple Wedger** or *Toasted Canapé Bread Slices.*

Yield: 18 servings (about 2 1/4 cups spread)

Nutrients per serving (2 tablespoons spread): Calories 120, Fat 11 g, Sodium 130 mg, Dietary Fiber 0 g

Toasted Canapé Bread Slices

1   package (11 ounces) refrigerated
     French bread dough

Preheat oven to 375°F. Using **Kitchen Spritzer**, lightly spray inside of **Bread Tube** and caps with vegetable oil. Cap bottom of Bread Tube; fill tube with dough. Place cap on top. Bake, upright, 50-60 minutes. Cool 10 minutes. Remove bread from tube onto **Nonstick Cooling Rack**. Cool completely. *Reduce oven temperature to 350°F.* Cut bread into 1/4-inch slices with **Serrated Bread Knife**. Arrange slices in single layer on flat **Baking Stone**. Bake 10-12 minutes or until light golden brown. Cool.

Yield: 24 slices

Nutrients per serving (1 slice): Calories 30, Fat 0 g, Sodium 80 mg, Dietary Fiber less than 1 g

Hot 'N Spicy Buffalo Wings

Originating in Buffalo, New York, this chicken wing appetizer is traditionally deep-fried.
Our version features the same spicy flavors, but is easier to prepare.

32 chicken wingettes or drummettes
   (about 3 pounds)
3/4 cup ketchup
3-4 tablespoons Tabasco® pepper
   sauce
3 tablespoons white vinegar
4 garlic cloves, pressed
4 stalks celery, cut into sticks
1 cup blue cheese salad dressing

Preheat oven to 375°F. Cut a 12 x 17-inch piece of **Parchment Paper** and press into bottom and up sides of **Stoneware Bar Pan**. Rinse chicken wingettes; pat dry with paper towels. In **1-Qt. Batter Bowl**, mix ketchup, pepper sauce and vinegar using **10" Whisk**. Press garlic into ketchup mixture using **Garlic Press**; mix well. Dip chicken into ketchup mixture; arrange in pan. Bake 45-50 minutes or until chicken is tender. Cut celery into sticks. Using **Nylon Tongs**, remove chicken to paper towels to drain. Serve hot with celery sticks and dressing.

Yield: 16 servings

Nutrients per serving (2 wingettes, 3 celery sticks and 1 tablespoon dressing): Calories 350, Fat 25 g, Sodium 370 mg, Dietary Fiber 0 g

Sausage Wrap-Arounds

We've added cornmeal crunch and tangy mustard for a new twist to this favorite snack.
When dipped in warm maple syrup, these are a favorite with kids.

1 tablespoon cornmeal
1 package (11 ounces) refrigerated
   bread sticks
2 tablespoons Dijon mustard
24 fully cooked small smoked
   sausage links
1/2 cup maple-flavored syrup, warmed

Preheat oven to 375°F. Sprinkle **13" x 9" Cutting Board** with cornmeal. Unroll bread stick dough over cornmeal; spread evenly with mustard using **Skinny Scraper**. Using **Pizza Cutter**, cut dough along perforations to form 12 strips; diagonally cut each strip in half lengthwise to make 24 long, thin triangles. Place one sausage on short side of each triangle; roll up and place, point down, on **15" Round Baking Stone**. Bake 14-16 minutes or until golden brown. Serve with warm syrup for dipping.

Yield: 24 wraps

Nutrients per serving (2 wraps and 2 teaspoons syrup): Calories 170, Fat 4.5 g, Sodium 470 mg, Dietary Fiber 0 g

Touchdown Taco Dip

One chip will lead to another when you try this spicy bean dip.

1   can (16 ounces) refried beans
1   package (8 ounces) cream
      cheese, softened
1   cup sour cream
2   tablespoons taco seasoning mix
2   garlic cloves, pressed
2   ounces cheddar cheese,
      shredded (1/2 cup)
1/2   cup pitted ripe olives, chopped
2   tablespoons fresh cilantro or
      parsley, snipped
1   medium tomato, seeded and
      chopped
1/4   cup thinly sliced green onions
      with tops

Preheat oven to 350°F. Spread refried beans over bottom of **Deep Dish Baker** using **Super Scraper**. In **Classic 2-Qt. Batter Bowl**, combine cream cheese, sour cream and taco seasoning. Press garlic into Batter Bowl using **Garlic Press**; mix well. Spread over beans. Shred cheese over top using **Deluxe Cheese Grater**. Bake 15-18 minutes or until hot. Chop olives using **Food Chopper**. Snip cilantro using **Kitchen Shears**. Sprinkle tomato, onions, olives and cilantro over dip. Garnish with additional sour cream, if desired. Serve with *Baked Tortilla Chips*.

Yield: 16 servings

Nutrients per serving (1/4 cup dip): Calories 140, Fat 10 g, Sodium 310 mg, Dietary Fiber 2 g

Baked Tortilla Chips

8   (7-inch) flour tortillas

Preheat oven to 400°F. Using **Pizza Cutter**, cut each tortilla into 8 wedges; arrange half of tortilla wedges in single layer on flat **Baking Stone**. Bake 6-8 minutes or until edges are lightly browned and crisp. Remove from Baking Stone; cool completely. Repeat with remaining tortilla wedges.

Yield: 64 chips

Nutrients per serving (4 chips): Calories 40, Fat 1 g, Sodium 130 mg, Dietary Fiber less than 1 g

Flaky Crabmeat Bundles

*A delicate crabmeat filling is encased in crisp layers of phyllo
then served with a gingered soy and sesame sauce.*

Bundles

- 2 cans (6 ounces each) lump crabmeat, drained
- 1 container (8 ounces) chive & onion soft cream cheese
- 2/3 cup fresh pea pods or sugar-snap peas, coarsely chopped
- 1/4 teaspoon salt
- 1 medium carrot, shredded (1/2 cup)
- 2 garlic cloves, pressed
- 6 sheets frozen phyllo pastry, thawed
- 2 tablespoons vegetable oil

Sauce

- 1/2 cup light soy sauce
- 1/4 cup balsamic or white wine vinegar
- 2 teaspoons peeled fresh ginger root, finely chopped
- 2 teaspoons sesame oil

Preheat oven to 375°F. For bundles, combine crabmeat, cream cheese, pea pods and salt in **1-Qt. Batter Bowl**. Using **Deluxe Cheese Grater**, shred carrot. Add carrot to Batter Bowl along with garlic pressed with **Garlic Press**; mix well. Place an 18-inch long piece of **Parchment Paper** on flat side of **18" x 12" Grooved Cutting Board**. Unfold one phyllo sheet onto parchment paper. (Keep remaining phyllo sheets covered with plastic wrap.) Using **Kitchen Spritzer** filled with vegetable oil, generously spray phyllo sheet. Top with second phyllo sheet; spray with oil. Repeat with third sheet of phyllo and oil. Trim phyllo sheets to a 16 x 12-inch rectangle using **5" Utility Knife**. Cut through all layers of phyllo to make twelve 4-inch squares. Using small **Stainless Steel Scoop**, drop rounded scoops of crabmeat mixture onto center of each square. For each bundle, bring four corners together at top; pinch. Place bundles on flat **Baking Stone**. Bake 15 minutes or until edges are golden brown. Remove from oven; place on **Nonstick Cooling Rack**. Repeat with remaining phyllo sheets and crabmeat mixture to make 24 bundles. For sauce, combine all ingredients in **Measure, Mix, & Pour™**; mix well. Serve warm bundles with sauce.

Yield: 24 bundles, 3/4 cup sauce

Nutrients per serving (1 bundle and 1 1/2 teaspoons sauce): Calories 80, Fat 5 g, Sodium 350 mg, Dietary Fiber 0 g

COOK'S TIP

- *Phyllo, a Greek word meaning "leaves", is pastry dough that is rolled into very thin sheets. It is used for a variety of pastries and appetizers and can be found in the frozen food section of most grocery stores. You should keep frozen phyllo wrapped when thawing in the refrigerator. Phyllo pastry dries out very quickly so the package should not be opened until the filling for Flaky Crabmeat Bundles is prepared.*

Lacy Cheese Rounds

Once your Baking Stone is well seasoned, it has the perfect nonstick coating needed for baking these delicate cheese "wafers".

1   package (8-ounce chunk)
     Monterey Jack or Colby cheese
1   container (8 ounces) refrigerated
     French onion, guacamole or
     ranch dip
1   medium tomato, seeded and
     chopped
     Fresh cilantro leaves or parsley
     sprigs

Preheat oven to 375°F. Cut cheese chunk (5½ x 2 inches) into ¼-inch slices; cut each slice in half to make squares. Place half of cheese squares 2 inches apart on **15" Round Baking Stone**. Bake 16-18 minutes or until cheese is lacy in appearance and edges are lightly browned. Cool cheese rounds 1 minute on Baking Stone until cheese stops sizzling. Remove with **Mini-Serving Spatula** to **Nonstick Cooling Rack**. Carefully wipe hot Baking Stone with paper towels; place remaining cheese squares on Baking Stone and bake as directed. Cool cheese rounds completely. Just before serving, attach **Open Star Tip** to **Easy Accent Decorator™**; fill with dip. Pipe dip onto cheese rounds. Garnish with tomato and cilantro.

Yield: 44 appetizers

Nutrients per serving (2 appetizers): Calories 60, Fat 5 g, Sodium 150 mg, Dietary Fiber less than 1 g

Golden Seafood Tart

Convenient refrigerated pie crusts bake up flaky around a cheesy filling of shrimp and vegetables for a delicious appetizer tart.

4   ounces cooked shrimp,
     chopped (⅔ cup)
½   cup broccoli, chopped
¼   cup celery, chopped
2   tablespoons onion, finely chopped
1   garlic clove, pressed
4   ounces Monterey Jack cheese,
     shredded (1 cup)
¼   cup mayonnaise
1   teaspoon Dijon mustard
     Dash ground black pepper
1   package (15 ounces) refrigerated
     pie crusts (2 crusts)
1   egg, lightly beaten

Preheat oven to 450°F. Using **Food Chopper**, chop shrimp, broccoli, celery and onion; place in **1-Qt. Batter Bowl**. Press garlic over shrimp mixture using **Garlic Press**. Shred cheese using **Deluxe Cheese Grater**. Add cheese, mayonnaise, mustard and black pepper to Batter Bowl; mix well. Place one pie crust on **13" Round Baking Stone**. Spread shrimp mixture over crust to within 1 inch of edge. Brush edge with egg using **Pastry Brush**. Top with remaining crust; pinch edges together. Turn sealed edge up and flute. Using **V-Shaped Cutter**, cut slits in top crust. Brush with remaining egg. Bake 20-25 minutes or until deep golden brown. Cut into wedges using **Slice 'N Serve®**.

Yield: 16 servings

Nutrients per Serving: Calories 180, Fat 12 g, Sodium 230 mg, Dietary Fiber 0 g

Broccoli Salad Squares

Familiar ingredients from a favorite salad are sprinkled over a golden baked crust for this garden-fresh appetizer.

1	package (8 ounces) refrigerated crescent rolls
3/4	cup mayonnaise
2	teaspoons sugar
1	teaspoon white or cider vinegar
1½	cups broccoli flowerets, chopped
4	slices bacon, crisply cooked and chopped
2	tablespoons red onion, thinly sliced and quartered
¼	cup golden raisins (optional)
1	tablespoon sunflower seed kernels

Preheat oven to 350°F. Unroll crescent roll dough; do not separate. Using lightly floured **Dough and Pizza Roller**, roll out dough on **12" x 15" Rectangle Baking Stone** to within 1 inch of edges of Baking Stone. Bake 12-15 minutes or until golden brown. Remove from oven. Cool completely. In **1-Qt. Batter Bowl**, mix mayonnaise, sugar and vinegar; set aside. Chop broccoli and bacon using **Food Chopper**. Cut thin slice of onion into quarters using **5" Utility Knife**; separate pieces. Spread mayonnaise mixture over top of crust using **Large Spreader**. Sprinkle with broccoli, bacon, onion, raisins and sunflower seed kernels. Serve immediately or refrigerate for up to 1 hour. Cut into 24 squares with **Pizza Cutter**; serve using **Mini-Serving Spatula**.

Yield: 12 servings

Nutrients per serving (2 squares): Calories 190, Fat 16 g, Sodium 330 mg, Dietary Fiber 0 g

TOOL TIP

- *Chopping ingredients is fast, easy and efficient with the **Food Chopper**. The rotating blades can chop foods coarsely or finely depending on the number of times you press down on the plunger. Use the Food Chopper to prepare ingredients for many of our recipes and to chop nuts for baked goods, vegetables for salads and salsas, croutons for crumb coatings, graham crackers and sandwich cookies for dessert crusts, and candy bars and hard candies for ice cream drinks and sundae toppings.*

Mediterranean Cheese Quesadillas

*Fresh basil leaves and tangy feta cheese add new flair
to a traditional Mexican-style snack.*

8   (7-inch) flour tortillas
1   garlic clove, pressed
3   firm plum tomatoes, sliced
1/3 cup pitted ripe olives, sliced
1/4 cup loosely packed fresh basil
     leaves, snipped, or 4 teaspoons
     dried basil leaves
2   cups (8 ounces) shredded
     mozzarella cheese, divided
1/2 cup (3 ounces) crumbled feta
     cheese
     Olive or vegetable oil

Preheat oven to 425°F. Place 4 flour tortillas on
15" Round Baking Stone. Using **Garlic Press**, press
garlic over tortillas; spread evenly. Using **Ultimate Slice
& Grate**, thinly slice tomatoes. Slice olives using **Egg
Slicer Plus®**. Snip basil leaves with **Kitchen Shears**.
Sprinkle each tortilla with 1/4 cup of the mozzarella
cheese. Top with equal amounts of tomatoes, ripe olives,
basil and feta cheese. Top each tortilla with 1/4 cup of
the remaining mozzarella cheese and a second tortilla.
Spray tops lightly with oil using **Kitchen Spritzer**. Bake
8-10 minutes or until tops are lightly browned. Cool
5 minutes. Cut each quesadilla into 6 wedges using
Pizza Cutter. Serve warm.

Yield: 24 appetizers

Nutrients per serving (2 appetizers): Calories 130, Fat 6 g,
Sodium 320 mg, Dietary Fiber 0 g

COOK'S TIP

■ *Feta cheese is a classic Greek cheese that is
cured in brine. Soft, white and crumbly, it has
a tangy flavor that is enjoyed in salads and
many cooked dishes.*

Caramel Corn Snack Mix

Once you start eating this candy-coated popcorn, pretzel and cereal mixture,
it's almost impossible to stop.

8   cups popped popcorn
4   cups oven-toasted rice cereal
       squares
2   cups miniature pretzel twists
1   cup pecan halves
1   cup packed brown sugar
½   cup butter or margarine
¼   cup light corn syrup
1   teaspoon vanilla
½   teaspoon baking soda

Preheat oven to 300°F. Combine popcorn, cereal, pretzels and pecans in **Rectangular Lid/Bowl**. Combine brown sugar, butter and corn syrup in **Generation II 2-Qt. Saucepan**. Cook and stir with **Bamboo Spoon** over medium heat until mixture comes to a boil over entire surface. Reduce heat to medium-low. Cook without stirring 5 minutes. (Mixture should continue to bubble gently over surface.) Remove saucepan from heat. Quickly stir in vanilla and baking soda, stirring carefully. Pour over popcorn mixture in Lid/Bowl, stirring until well coated. Bake 30 minutes, stirring after 15 minutes. Transfer popcorn mixture to large piece of **Parchment Paper**. Cool completely, breaking mixture into clusters as it cools.

Yield: 15 cups

Nutrients per serving (1 cup): Calories 220, Fat 11 g, Sodium 290 mg, Dietary Fiber less than 1 g

COOK'S TIP

■ *You can use a microwave popcorn product to shorten your preparation time. A reduced fat (light or natural) type of popcorn will produce the crispiest results in this snack mix.*

Bountiful Brunch

*In these "hurry-up" times,
a relaxed weekend meal is
a welcome change of pace.
Combine the best of breakfast
and lunch when you delight
family and friends with ham
and eggs in a braided crust or
a shrimp pasta pie. Surprise
them with giant cinnamon
buns or gooey pull-apart rolls
baked in a special shape. With
every dish you make, you'll
find stoneware is a cook's
best friend.*

Ham 'N Eggs Brunch Braid

Never has there been such an impressive way to serve scrambled eggs! The cream cheese keeps the eggs moist, even after baking in our golden braided crust.

4   ounces cream cheese
1/2 cup milk
8   eggs, divided
1/4 teaspoon salt
    Dash ground black pepper
1/4 cup red bell pepper, chopped
2   tablespoons sliced green onions
       with tops
1   teaspoon butter or margarine
2   packages (8 ounces each)
       refrigerated crescent rolls
1/4 pound thinly-sliced deli ham
2   ounces cheddar cheese,
       shredded (1/2 cup)

Preheat oven to 375°F. Place cream cheese and milk in **Classic 2-Qt. Batter Bowl**. Microwave on HIGH 1 minute. Whisk until smooth using **10" Whisk**. Separate 1 egg using **Egg Separator**; reserve egg white. Add the yolk and remaining 7 eggs, salt and black pepper to Batter Bowl; whisk to combine. Chop bell pepper using **Food Chopper**. Add bell pepper and onions to egg mixture. Melt butter in **Generation II 10" Frying Pan** over medium-low heat. Add egg mixture; cook, stirring occasionally, until eggs are set but still moist. Remove pan from heat.

Unroll 1 package of crescent dough; do not separate. Arrange longest side of dough across width of **12" x 15" Rectangle Baking Stone**. Repeat with remaining package of dough. Using **Dough and Pizza Roller**, roll dough to seal perforations. On longest sides of Baking Stone, cut dough into strips 1 1/2 inches apart, 3 inches deep using **3" Paring Knife** (there will be 6 inches in the center for the filling). Arrange ham evenly over middle of dough. Spoon eggs over ham. Shred cheddar cheese over eggs using **Deluxe Cheese Grater**. To braid, lift strips of dough across filling to meet in center, twisting each strip one turn. Continue alternating strips to form a braid. Brush lightly beaten egg white over dough using **Pastry Brush**. Bake 25-28 minutes or until deep golden brown. Cut into slices with **Slice 'N Serve**®.

Yield: 10 servings

Nutrients per serving: Calories 310, Fat 21 g, Sodium 820 mg, Dietary Fiber less than 1 g

Apple Cinnamon French Toast

Brunch is a breeze when you assemble this French toast the night before.
Just bake the next morning while the coffee is brewing.

1	loaf (8 ounces) French bread
6	eggs
1½	cups milk
8	tablespoons sugar, divided
1	teaspoon vanilla
⅛	teaspoon salt
1½	teaspoons ground cinnamon
4	Granny Smith apples
2	tablespoons butter or margarine
	Maple-flavored syrup

Spray **9" x 13" Baker** with vegetable oil using **Kitchen Spritzer**. Cut bread into 1-inch-thick slices (10 -16 slices) using **Serrated Bread Knife**; arrange closely in single layer in Baker. In **Classic 2-Qt. Batter Bowl**, beat eggs with **10" Whisk**. Whisk in milk, 3 tablespoons of the sugar, vanilla and salt. Pour over bread. Combine the remaining 5 tablespoons sugar and cinnamon in **Flour/Sugar Shaker**. Peel, core and slice apples using **Apple Peeler/Corer/Slicer**. Cut into rings by slicing down one side of each apple with **3" Paring Knife**. Place half of apples over bread. Sprinkle half of the sugar-cinnamon mixture evenly over apples. Repeat layers. Cover and refrigerate 1 hour or overnight. Preheat oven to 400°F. Cut butter into small pieces and arrange over apples. Bake, uncovered, 30-35 minutes or until apples are tender. Let stand 5 minutes before serving. Serve with syrup.

Yield: 8 servings

Nutrients per serving (2 slices French toast and 2 tablespoons syrup):
Calories 370, Fat 9 g, Sodium 310 mg, Dietary Fiber 2 g

COOK'S TIP

■ French bread loaves come in a variety of sizes. If using a very thin loaf, cut slices on the diagonal.

TOOL TIP

■ Did you know? You can use the **Apple Peeler/Corer/Slicer** on potatoes to prepare oven-baked curly fries. This tool works best with fresh, firm, uniformly-shaped apples and potatoes.

Berry Pancake Puff

An oven-baked pancake gets its puffiness from the steam produced as the batter bakes. The fresh berry topping finishes this impressive breakfast delight.

Berry Topping

- 3 cups (any combination) fresh berries such as raspberries, blueberries, blackberries or sliced hulled strawberries
- 1/3 cup orange marmalade

Pancake

- 3 tablespoons butter or margarine, melted, divided
- 1 cup milk
- 6 eggs
- 1 cup all-purpose flour
- 1/2 teaspoon salt
- 2 tablespoons powdered sugar

Preheat oven to 450°F. For berry topping, gently stir together berries and marmalade in **1-Qt. Batter Bowl**; set aside. For pancake, use **Pastry Brush** to coat **Deep Dish Baker** with 1 tablespoon of the butter. In **Classic 2-Qt. Batter Bowl**, combine milk, eggs and remaining 2 tablespoons butter using **10" Whisk**. Slowly whisk in combined flour and salt until egg mixture is smooth. Pour batter into Baker. Bake 13 minutes. *Reduce oven temperature to 350°F* and continue baking 15-17 minutes or until sides are crisp and golden brown. Remove pancake from oven; immediately sprinkle with powdered sugar using **Flour/Sugar Shaker**. Fill center with berry topping. Cut into wedges using **Slice 'N Serve®**. Serve immediately.

Yield: 4 servings

Nutrients per serving: Calories 440, Fat 18 g, Sodium 500 mg, Dietary Fiber 4 g

TOOL TIP

- *Use The Pampered Chef's versatile **Egg Slicer Plus®** to slice strawberries quickly and easily. It's also perfect for slicing kiwi, bananas, mushrooms and olives into uniform slices.*

Country Breakfast Bake

Even city folks will enjoy this hearty breakfast.

¼ cup green onions with tops, chopped
¼ cup red bell pepper, chopped
3 cups frozen Southern-style hash brown potatoes
4 slices bacon, partially cooked, cut up
3 tablespoons vegetable oil or bacon drippings
4 eggs
   Salt and ground black pepper to taste
2 ounces Colby & Monterey Jack cheese blend, shredded (½ cup)

Preheat oven to 450°F. Chop onions and bell pepper using **Food Chopper**; place in **9" Square Baker**. Add potatoes, bacon and oil; mix well and spread evenly over bottom of Baker. Bake 20 minutes, stirring potato mixture after 10 minutes. *Reduce oven temperature to 325°F.* Remove Baker from oven and make 4 impressions in potato mixture with back of **Bamboo Spoon**. Break an egg into each impression. Sprinkle with salt and black pepper. Return to oven; continue baking 15 minutes or until eggs are set. Remove from oven. Using **Deluxe Cheese Grater**, shred cheese evenly over eggs.

Yield: 4 servings

Nutrients per serving: Calories 350, Fat 22 g, Sodium 320 mg, Dietary Fiber 2 g

 COOK'S TIP

 TOOL TIP

■ *Recipe can be doubled and baked in the* **9" x 13" Baker**.

■ *After chopping green onions and bell pepper, use the* **Kitchen Scraper** *to easily transfer vegetables from the cutting board to the Baker.*

Country Breakfast Bake

Brunch

Garden Fresh Oven Omelet

Summer's bountiful supply of fresh zucchini is featured in this easy, deep-dish vegetable pie.

2   medium baking potatoes
      (about 1 pound)
¼   cup onion, finely chopped
4   ounces cheddar cheese,
      shredded (1 cup)
1   cup zucchini, thinly sliced
6   eggs
1   cup milk
¼   cup all-purpose flour
¾   teaspoon salt
⅛   teaspoon ground black pepper
1   medium tomato, seeded and
      chopped

Preheat oven to 400°F. Lightly spray **Deep Dish Baker** with vegetable oil using **Kitchen Spritzer**. Peel and slice potatoes using **Apple Peeler/Corer/Slicer**. Using **Food Chopper**, coarsely chop potato slices, potato cores and onion; place in bottom of Baker. Using **Deluxe Cheese Grater**, shred cheese over onion and potatoes. Slice zucchini with **Ultimate Slice & Grate**; arrange evenly over cheese. In **Classic 2-Qt. Batter Bowl**, whisk eggs, milk, flour, salt and pepper with **10" Whisk**. Pour egg mixture over vegetables and cheese. Bake 30-35 minutes or until knife inserted in center comes out clean. Sprinkle tomatoes over omelet. Let stand 5 minutes. Cut and serve using **Slice 'N Serve®**.

Yield: 8 servings

Nutrients per serving: Calories 170, Fat 10 g, Sodium 360 mg, Dietary Fiber 1 g

COOK'S TIP

■ *Recipe can be prepared using the **9" x 13" Baker**. Use 3 medium baking potatoes (about 1½ pounds), ⅓ cup chopped onion, 6 ounces (1½ cups) shredded cheese, 1½ cups sliced zucchini, 8 eggs, 1½ cups milk, ⅓ cup flour, 1 teaspoon salt, ¼ teaspoon ground black pepper and 1 large tomato. Yield: 12 servings*

Chicken Artichoke &
Rice Casserole

A well-seasoned white and wild rice mix is the start to this special dish.
Serve it with a green salad or fresh fruit.

1   package (6.2 ounces) fast-cooking
     long-grain and wild rice mix (plus
     ingredients to make rice)
1   medium red bell pepper
1   can (14 ounces) artichoke hearts
     in water
3   cups chopped cooked chicken
1/4   cup sliced green onions with tops
1   jar (12 ounces) chicken gravy
1/2   cup sour cream
4   ounces cheddar cheese,
     shredded (1 cup)

Preheat oven to 350°F. Prepare rice mix according to package directions in **Generation II 3-Qt. Saucepan**. Remove saucepan from heat. Slice bell pepper using **8" Chef's Knife** to make three rings for garnish; set rings aside. Chop remaining bell pepper. Drain artichokes in **1-Qt. Colander**; cut into bite-size pieces. Add chopped bell pepper, artichokes, chicken and green onions to rice; mix well and spoon into **9" Square Baker**. In **1-Qt. Batter Bowl**, mix gravy and sour cream until blended. Shred cheese into Batter Bowl using **Deluxe Cheese Grater**; mix well. Spread gravy mixture over rice mixture using **Super Scraper**. Bake 25-27 minutes or until thoroughly heated. Garnish with bell pepper rings; sprinkle with additional sliced green onions, if desired.

Yield: 8 servings

Nutrients per serving: Calories 350, Fat 17 g, Sodium 690 mg, Dietary Fiber 4 g

COOK'S TIP

■ *A fast-cooking rice mix saves preparation time but if you prefer rice with firmer texture, use a conventionally prepared rice mix (with a cooking time of 20-25 minutes).*

Peanutty Chocolate Banana Bread

Use very ripe bananas for the sweetest flavor.
This bread has definite a-peel!

2	cups all-purpose flour
1	cup sugar
1	tablespoon baking powder
1/2	teaspoon salt
1	cup mashed ripe bananas (about 2 medium)
1/3	cup milk
1/3	cup peanut butter
3	tablespoons vegetable oil
1	egg
1	cup milk chocolate morsels, divided
1/3	cup peanuts, chopped

Preheat oven to 350°F. Spray bottom only of **Stoneware Loaf Pan** with vegetable oil using **Kitchen Spritzer**. In **Classic 2-Qt. Batter Bowl**, combine flour, sugar, baking powder and salt. Add bananas, milk, peanut butter, oil and egg; stir just until dry ingredients are moistened using **Mix 'N Scraper®**. Stir in 3/4 cup of the milk chocolate morsels. Spoon batter into pan. Using **Food Chopper**, coarsely chop peanuts. Sprinkle peanuts and remaining 1/4 cup milk chocolate morsels evenly over batter. Bake 60 minutes or until **Cake Tester** inserted in center comes out clean. Cool in pan 10 minutes. Loosen sides of loaf from pan; remove loaf to **Nonstick Cooling Rack**. Cool completely. Cut into slices using **Serrated Bread Knife**.

Yield: 1 loaf (12 servings)

Nutrients per serving (1 slice): Calories 320, Fat 14 g, Sodium 190 mg, Dietary Fiber 2 g

TOOL TIPS

■ The **Measure-All™ Cup** is the ideal tool for measuring peanut butter. Its unique plunger design allows foods to eject cleanly from the cup with little cleanup.

■ Use the **Nylon Masher** to mash bananas.

Peanutty Chocolate Banana Bread

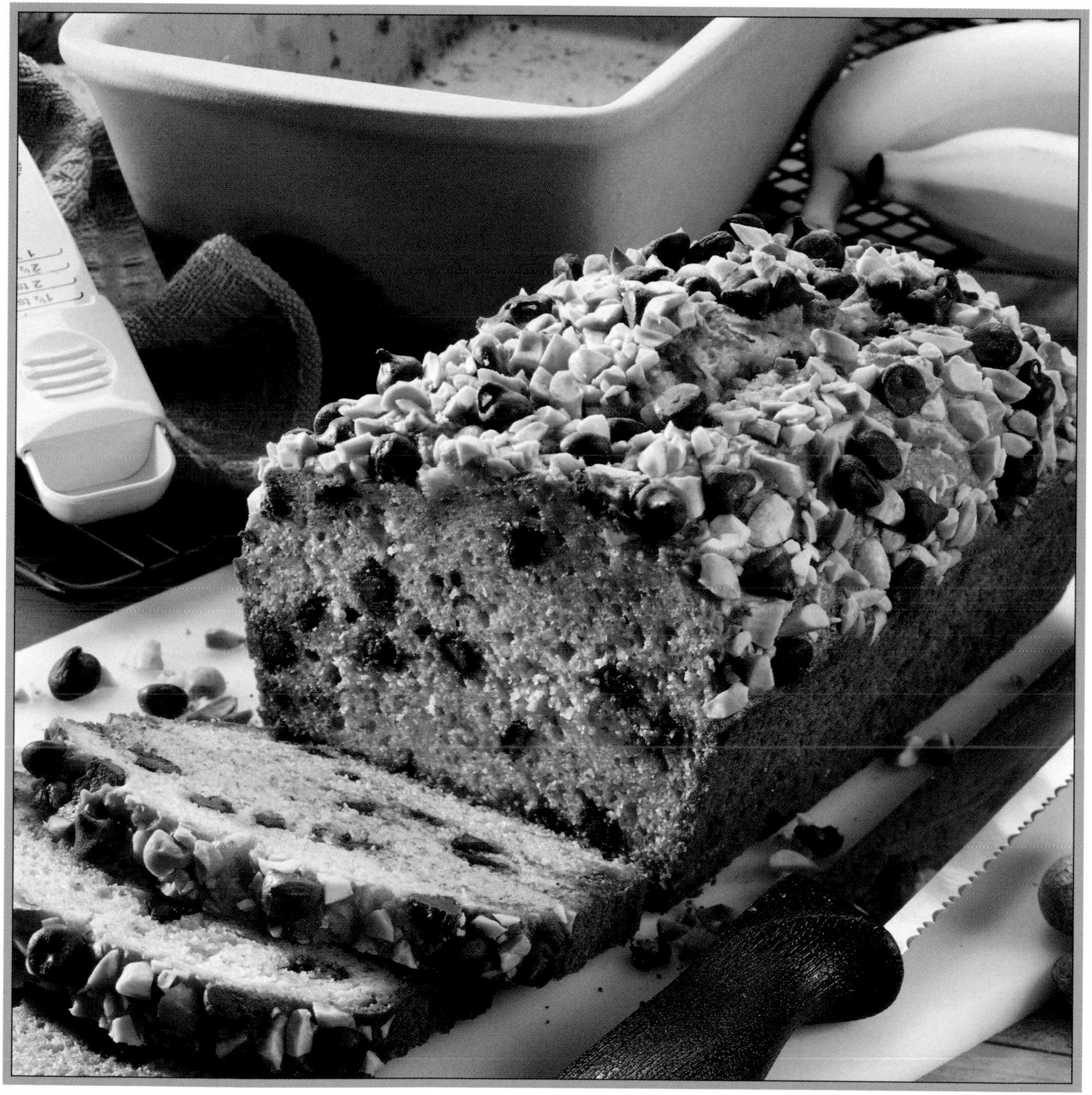

Spiced Carrot-Zucchini Bread

Pictured on p. 2

*With flecks of orange and green, this fragrant quick bread
is perfect for breakfast or tea time.*

2¼	cups all-purpose flour
1	cup sugar
¾	teaspoon baking soda
½	teaspoon baking powder
½	teaspoon salt
1½	teaspoons ground cinnamon
¼	teaspoon ground cloves
¾	cup carrots, finely chopped
¾	cup zucchini, finely chopped
½	cup walnuts, coarsely chopped
⅔	cup vegetable oil
½	cup milk
2	eggs

Preheat oven to 350°F. Spray bottom only of **Stoneware Loaf Pan** with nonstick cooking spray. In **Classic 2-Qt. Batter Bowl**, combine flour, sugar, baking soda, baking powder, salt and spices. Using **Food Chopper**, finely chop carrots and zucchini; coarsely chop walnuts. Add carrots, zucchini, walnuts and remaining ingredients to Batter Bowl. Stir just until dry ingredients are moistened using **Mix 'N Scraper®**. Spoon batter into pan. Bake 65-70 minutes or until **Cake Tester** inserted in center comes out clean. Cool in pan 5 minutes. Loosen sides of loaf from pan; remove loaf to **Nonstick Cooling Rack**. Cool completely. Cut into slices using **Serrated Bread Knife**.

Yield: 1 loaf (12 servings)

Nutrients per serving (1 slice): Calories 300, Fat 16 g, Sodium 200 mg, Dietary Fiber 1 g

COOK'S TIP

■ *The Pampered Chef Pantry™ Korintje **Cinnamon** can be substituted for ground cinnamon.*

TOOL TIPS

■ *The **Mix 'N Scraper®** is a heavy-duty spatula designed to easily mix thick batters.*

■ *Peel carrots quicker than ever by using our **Vegetable Peeler** featuring a unique, swivel-action blade.*

Twice-As-Nice Danish Braids

*With a different fruity filling in each, these two braids bake
side by side on the Rectangle Baking Stone.*

Braids

- 1 package (8 ounces) cream cheese, softened
- ¼ cup sugar
- ½ teaspoon almond extract
- 1 egg, separated
- 2 packages (8 ounces each) refrigerated crescent rolls
- 3 tablespoons seedless raspberry jam
- 3 tablespoons peach preserves

Streusel

- ⅓ cup all-purpose flour
- 2 tablespoons sugar
- 2 tablespoons natural whole almonds, chopped
- 2 tablespoons butter or margarine, melted

Preheat oven to 375°F. For braids, mix cream cheese, sugar and almond extract. Separate egg using **Egg Separator**; reserve egg white. Add egg yolk to cream cheese mixture, mixing until smooth. Unroll 1 package of crescent roll dough; do not separate. Arrange longest side of dough across width of one end of **12" x 15" Rectangle Baking Stone**. Using **Dough and Pizza Roller**, roll dough to seal perforations. Spread half of the cream cheese mixture in 3-inch strip lengthwise down center of dough to within ¼ inch of each end. Carefully spread raspberry jam over cream cheese mixture using **Skinny Scraper**. Using **3" Paring Knife**, make cuts along sides of dough 1½ inches apart to within ½ inch of filling. To braid, lift strips of dough across filling to meet in center, twisting each strip one turn. Continue alternating strips to form a braid. Fold up ends of braid to seal. Repeat procedure on opposite end of Baking Stone with remaining crescent roll dough, cream cheese mixture and peach preserves to make a second braid. Brush lightly beaten egg white over dough using **Pastry Brush**. For streusel, mix flour, sugar, almonds and butter until crumbly. Sprinkle evenly over braids, patting gently. Bake 22-25 minutes or until deep golden brown. Cut into slices with **Slice 'N Serve®**.

Yield: 2 coffee cakes (10 servings)

Nutrients per serving: Calories 350, Fat 21 g, Sodium 450 mg, Dietary Fiber less than 1 g

COOK'S TIP

- *Any favorite fruit jam or preserves may be substituted for raspberry jam or peach preserves.*

Giant Cinnamon Rolls

Warm, gooey and loaded with cinnamon, these rolls are even better than ones from the bakery. Using a hot roll mix, usually found in the baking section of the supermarket, is a great shortcut.

Dough

1	package (16 ounces) hot roll mix (including yeast packet)
2	tablespoons granulated sugar
1	cup hot water (120°- 130°F)
2	tablespoons butter or margarine, softened
1	egg

Filling

1/4	cup butter or margarine, softened
1/4	cup granulated sugar
1/4	cup packed brown sugar
2	tablespoons ground cinnamon
1	tablespoon light corn syrup

Frosting

2	ounces cream cheese, softened
2	tablespoons butter or margarine, softened
1/2	teaspoon vanilla
1 1/3	cups powdered sugar
1	tablespoon milk

For dough, combine hot roll mix, yeast packet and sugar in **Classic 2-Qt. Batter Bowl**. Stir in hot water, butter and egg until dough pulls away from side of bowl. Turn dough out onto lightly floured flat side of **18" x 12" Grooved Cutting Board**. With floured hands, shape dough into a ball. Knead dough 5 minutes until smooth. Cover with Batter Bowl; let rest 5 minutes. Using lightly floured **Dough and Pizza Roller**, roll dough into a 15 x 10-inch rectangle. For filling, combine butter, sugars, cinnamon and corn syrup; mix well. (Mixture will be stiff.) Spread over dough using **Skinny Scraper** to within 1/2 inch of edges. Starting at one short side, roll up tightly; press edge to seal. Slice evenly into 6 slices; place in **9" x 13" Baker**. Cover loosely with plastic wrap and cloth towel. Let rise in warm place (80°- 85°F) 30 minutes. Preheat oven to 325°F. Uncover rolls. Bake 30-35 minutes or until golden brown. Cool rolls in Baker 15 minutes. For frosting, combine cream cheese, butter and vanilla in **1-Qt. Batter Bowl**. Whisk in powdered sugar and milk using **10" Whisk** until smooth. Spread over warm rolls using **All-Purpose Spreader**.

Yield: 6 rolls

Nutrients per serving: Calories 560, Fat 14 g, Sodium 650 mg, Dietary Fiber 3 g

COOK'S TIPS

- To make slightly smaller rolls, slice dough evenly into 8 slices.

- There are several ways to create a warm place for rolls to rise. One method is to place the **9" x 13" Baker** on a rack over a large bowl filled with very hot tap water. Another way is to turn your oven on to the lowest setting for one minute; turn oven off. Place Baker on center rack and close oven door.

- To make rolls ahead, after placing rolls in Baker, cover loosely with plastic wrap and refrigerate overnight. Remove Baker from refrigerator. Let stand at room temperature 15 minutes. Let rise and bake as directed.

Cinnamon Orange Pull-Aparts

Some people call this type of breakfast treat "Monkey Bread".
Maybe because it's so fun to shape, roll and eat.

1	orange
3/4	cup sugar
1 1/2	teaspoons ground cinnamon
5	tablespoons butter or margarine, melted
18	frozen bread dough rolls, thawed (1/2 of 48-ounce package)
1/3	cup light corn syrup, divided

Spray **Stoneware Fluted Pan** with vegetable oil using **Kitchen Spritzer**. Zest orange using **Lemon Zester/Scorer** to measure 1 tablespoon zest. In **1-Qt. Batter Bowl**, combine sugar, cinnamon and zest; mix well. In **Covered Micro-Cooker®**, microwave butter on HIGH 30 seconds or until melted. Cut each roll in half using **Kitchen Shears**. Dip half of the cut rolls in butter; roll in sugar mixture to coat. Arrange in pan. Drizzle with half of the corn syrup. Repeat with remaining rolls and corn syrup; sprinkle any remaining sugar mixture over rolls. Cover loosely with plastic wrap and cloth towel. Let rise in warm place (80°-85°F) until double in size, about 1 hour. Preheat oven to 350°F. Uncover; bake 30-35 minutes or until top is deep golden brown. Cool in pan on **Nonstick Cooling Rack** 5 minutes. Carefully invert onto serving plate. To serve, pull apart or slice using **Serrated Bread Knife**.

Yield: 16 servings

Nutrients per serving: Calories 210, Fat 6 g, Sodium 280 mg, Dietary Fiber 1 g

COOK'S TIPS

■ *There are several ways to create a warm place for dough to rise. One method is to place the* **Fluted Pan** *on a rack over a large pan filled with hot tap water. A second way is to turn your oven on to the lowest setting for one minute; turn oven off. Place Fluted Pan on center rack and close oven door.*

■ *To make ahead, after placing rolls in Fluted Pan, cover loosely with plastic wrap and refrigerate overnight. Remove from refrigerator. Let stand at room temperature 15 minutes. Let rise and bake as directed.*

■ *The Pampered Chef Pantry™ Korintje Cinnamon can be substituted for the ground cinnamon.*

Mom's Apple Noodle Kugel

Kugel is a traditional Jewish side dish. With apples and raisins, our version of this special baked noodle pudding would be equally delicious served for dessert.

1　package (8 ounces) cream
　　cheese, softened
¹/4　cup plus 1 tablespoon butter,
　　melted, divided
4　eggs
1　cup sour cream
¹/2　cup milk
¹/3　cup plus 2 teaspoons sugar,
　　divided
³/4　teaspoon ground cinnamon,
　　divided
¹/4　teaspoon salt
2　medium apples, chopped
　　(2 cups)
6　ounces (about 3¹/2 cups)
　　uncooked medium egg
　　noodles, cooked and drained
¹/2　cup raisins
2　cups corn flake cereal

Preheat oven to 350°F. Lightly spray bottom of **9" Square Baker** with vegetable oil using **Kitchen Spritzer**. Place cream cheese in **4-Qt. Bowl**. Gradually whisk in ¹/4 cup of the melted butter using **10" Whisk**. Whisk in eggs. Mix in sour cream, milk, ¹/3 cup of the sugar, ¹/2 teaspoon of the cinnamon and salt. Chop apples using **Food Chopper**. Fold cooked noodles, apples and raisins into cream cheese mixture using **Mix 'N Scraper®**. Pour into Baker. Coarsely crush corn flakes in large, resealable plastic bag using **Dough and Pizza Roller**. Add remaining 1 tablespoon melted butter to bag and mix lightly. Sprinkle cereal mixture over noodles. Combine remaining 2 teaspoons sugar and ¹/4 teaspoon cinnamon in **Flour/Sugar Shaker**. Sprinkle over cereal. Bake 35-40 minutes or until set. Let stand 10 minutes before serving.

Yield: 12 servings

Nutrients per serving: Calories 310, Fat 18 g, Sodium 240 mg, Dietary Fiber 1 g

COOK'S TIP

■ *Use apples with red skins to add color to your noodle kugel.*

Apricot Almond Coffee Cake

*Golden dried apricots and crunchy almonds are simple additions to a pound cake mix.
Coffee cakes bake to a beautiful shape in our Stoneware Fluted Pan.*

Cake

3/4	cup dried apricots, chopped
1/2	cup slivered almonds
1	tablespoon all-purpose flour
1	package (16 ounces) pound cake mix (plus ingredients to make cake)

Glaze

1	cup powdered sugar
4-5	teaspoons milk
1/4	teaspoon almond extract (optional)

Preheat oven to 325°F. Spray **Stoneware Fluted Pan** with nonstick cooking spray. For cake, chop apricots using **Food Chopper**. In **1-Qt. Batter Bowl**, mix apricots, almonds and flour; set aside. In **Classic 2-Qt. Batter Bowl**, prepare cake mix according to package directions. Gently stir in apricot mixture. Spread batter evenly in pan. Bake 55-65 minutes or until **Cake Tester** inserted near center comes out clean. Cool in pan on **Nonstick Cooling Rack** 10 minutes; loosen cake from edge and center of pan with knife. Invert onto rack. Cool 20 minutes. For glaze, combine powdered sugar, milk and extract, if desired; drizzle over warm cake. Serve warm or at room temperature using **Serrated Bread Knife** to slice.

Yield: 12 servings

Nutrients per serving: Calories 300, Fat 9 g, Sodium 180 mg, Dietary Fiber 1 g

COOK'S TIP

- *For extra flavor, toast almonds in **8" Mini-Baker** at 325°F for 12-15 minutes or until lightly browned. Cool before mixing with apricots.*

TOOL TIP

- *Use the **V-Shaped Cutter** to drizzle glaze over top of coffee cake.*

Brunch

Shrimp Pasta Pie

A creamy Parmesan cheese sauce perfectly complements pasta, shrimp and broccoli in this special brunch dish. Round out your meal with fresh fruit and rolls.

8   ounces uncooked thin spaghetti,
      cooked and drained
4   tablespoons butter or margarine,
      divided
3   eggs, lightly beaten
1/4 teaspoon ground black pepper
2   ounces fresh Parmesan cheese,
      grated (about 1/2 cup)
1   garlic clove, pressed
1 1/2 cups small broccoli flowerets
1/2 cup chopped red bell pepper
1/3 cup sliced green onions with tops
8   ounces uncooked, medium fresh
      shrimp, peeled and deveined
1   container (10 ounces) refrigerated
      Alfredo pasta sauce, divided
2   ounces mozzarella cheese,
      shredded (1/2 cup)

Preheat oven to 350°F. Spray **Deep Dish Baker** with vegetable oil using **Kitchen Spritzer**. Cook spaghetti according to package directions in **Generation II 6-Qt. Dutch Oven**; drain in **5 1/4-Qt. Colander**. Transfer to **4-Qt. Bowl**. Add 3 tablespoons of the butter, cut into small pieces; stir until melted using **Nylon Slotted Server**. Add eggs and black pepper. Grate Parmesan cheese over pasta using **Deluxe Cheese Grater**; mix well. Spoon into Baker. Spread mixture evenly, forming a 1-inch rim around edge of Baker to make a shell. Bake 10-12 minutes or until set.

Melt remaining 1 tablespoon butter in **Generation II Stir-Fry Skillet** over medium-high heat. Press garlic into skillet using **Garlic Press**. Add vegetables and shrimp; stir-fry 4 minutes or until shrimp is opaque. Remove skillet from heat. Stir in 1/2 cup of the pasta sauce. Spoon shrimp mixture into pasta shell. Shred mozzarella cheese over shrimp mixture using Deluxe Cheese Grater. Bake 10 minutes. Let stand 5 minutes. Cut into wedges and serve using **Slice 'N Serve®**. Heat remaining sauce in **Covered Micro-Cooker®** on MEDIUM 2-3 minutes or until hot, stirring every minute. Serve over pasta.

Yield: 8 servings

Nutrients per serving: Calories 320, Fat 24 g, Sodium 610 mg, Dietary Fiber less than 1 g

COOK'S TIP

■ *Frozen uncooked shrimp, thawed according to package directions, can be substituted for fresh shrimp.*

TOOL TIP

■ *The **Deluxe Cheese Grater** comes with a grating drum for grating the Parmesan cheese and a shredding drum for shredding the mozzarella cheese.*

Shrimp Pasta Pie

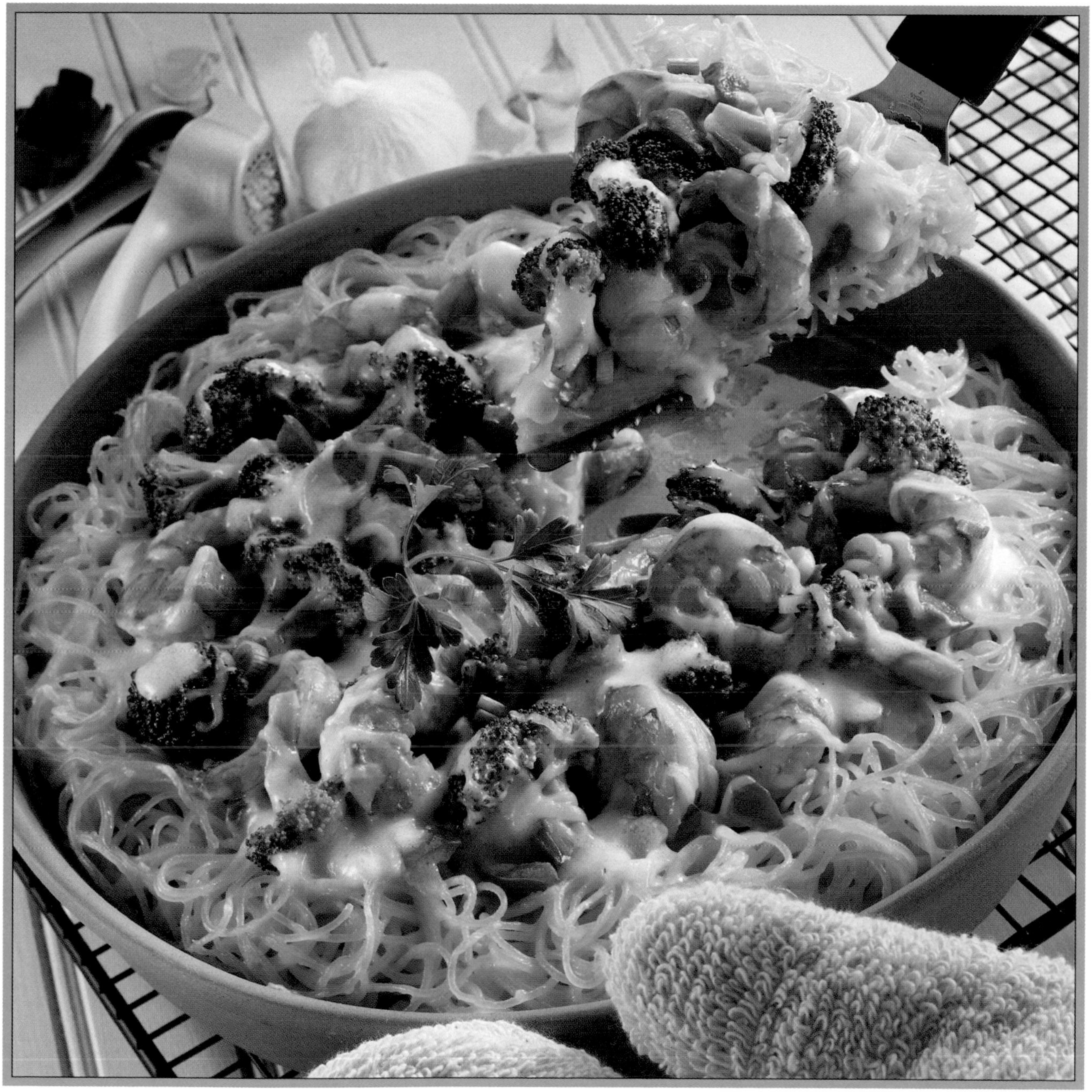

Marvelous Main Dishes

For help with everyday meals or special dinners, turn to The Family Heritage® Stoneware Collection. Many stoneware pieces have been specially designed to work together, just right for roasting meats and poultry to tender, juicy perfection. You'll find casseroles heat evenly and pizza crusts bake beautifully when using our stoneware. Turn the page to discover how these marvelous main dishes can become the centerpieces for family mealtimes.

Company Roast Chicken

Garlic-herb butter rubbed under the skin makes this roasting chicken extra flavorful. Baking poultry in the combination Stoneware Baker and Rectangular Lid/Bowl makes it extra moist.

3/4	cup natural whole almonds, coarsely chopped
6	cups cooked converted long-grain white rice
3/4	cup golden raisins
1/4	cup snipped fresh parsley, divided
1/4	cup fresh thyme leaves or 4 teaspoons dried thyme leaves, divided
3	tablespoons sliced green onions with tops
2	garlic cloves, pressed
1/4	cup butter or margarine, softened
1	roasting chicken (5½-6½ pounds)

Preheat oven to 400°F. For rice mixture, coarsely chop almonds using **Food Chopper**; place in **Classic 2-Qt. Batter Bowl**. Add cooked rice, raisins, 3 tablespoons of the parsley, 3 tablespoons of the fresh thyme leaves (or 3 teaspoons dried) and green onions; mix well. For garlic-herb butter, press garlic using **Garlic Press** into **1-Qt. Batter Bowl**. Add butter, remaining 1 tablespoon parsley and remaining 1 tablespoon fresh thyme leaves (or 1 teaspoon dried); mix well using **Skinny Scraper**. Remove and discard giblets and neck from chicken cavity. Rinse chicken with cold water; pat dry. Trim excess fat using **Kitchen Shears**, if necessary. Starting with neck cavity, loosen skin from breast by inserting fingers, gently pushing between skin and meat. Tie ends of legs together with cotton string. Lift wing tips up toward neck then tuck under back of chicken. Place chicken in **9" x 13" Baker**, breast side up. Slide butter mixture under skin of breast, using Skinny Scraper. Using fingers, press skin to evenly distribute butter mixture under skin. Fill cavity of chicken with 2 cups rice mixture. Place **Rectangular Lid/Bowl** over Baker. Spoon remaining rice mixture into **Mini-Baking Bowl**; cover with **8" Mini-Baker** and set aside. Bake chicken 1 hour. Carefully remove Lid/Bowl from Baker, lifting away from you. Place covered Mini-Baking Bowl in oven with chicken. Bake rice 20-25 minutes or until thoroughly heated. Continue baking chicken 15-30 minutes or until **Pocket Thermometer** registers 180°F in meaty part of thigh and juices run clear. Let stand 10 minutes before carving with **8" Chef's Knife**.

Yield: 8 servings

Nutrients per serving: Calories 650 , Fat 24 g, Sodium 190 mg, Dietary Fiber 3 g

All-American Cheeseburger Ring

Kids love the cheeseburgers at fast-food restaurants, so you're sure to bring out the smiles with this cheeseburger ring.

1/4	cup onion, chopped
3/4	pound lean (90%) ground beef
1/4	cup ketchup
2	teaspoons prepared yellow mustard
9	slices (3/4 ounce each) American cheese, divided
2	packages (8 ounces each) refrigerated crescent rolls
16	dill pickle slices
3	large plum tomatoes
2	cups lettuce, shredded

Preheat oven to 375°F. Chop onion using **Food Chopper**. In **Generation II 10" Frying Pan**, cook ground beef with onion over medium heat 8-10 minutes or until beef is no longer pink; drain. Add ketchup, mustard and 5 of the cheese slices, cut up; stir until cheese is melted. Remove pan from heat. Unroll crescent dough; separate into 16 triangles. Arrange triangles in a circle on **13" Round Baking Stone** with wide ends of triangles overlapping in the center and points toward the outside. (There should be a 5-inch diameter opening in center of Baking Stone.) Using medium **Stainless Steel Scoop**, scoop meat mixture evenly onto widest end of each triangle. Top each scoop with pickle slice. Bring points of triangles up over filling and tuck under wide ends of dough at center of ring. (Filling will not be completely covered.) Bake 20-25 minutes or until deep golden brown. Remove from oven. Using **Garnisher**, cut each of the remaining 4 cheese slices into 4 triangles. Arrange cheese triangles over top of ring. Slice tomatoes using **Ultimate Slice & Grate**. Arrange tomato slices around inside center of ring. Slice lettuce into thin strands using Garnisher. Place in center of ring. Cut ring into 8 servings using **Slice 'N Serve®**. Serve with additional ketchup and mustard, if desired.

Yield: 8 servings

Nutrients per serving: Calories 430, Fat 27 g, Sodium 1090 mg, Dietary Fiber 1 g

COOK'S TIP

- *Just for fun, use a green bell pepper "bowl" to hold your additional condiments. Using **5" Utility Knife**, cut a green bell pepper in half vertically being careful to keep the dividing inside membranes intact. Carefully remove seed pods. Reserve one half bell pepper for another use. Fill remaining pepper half (divided by membrane) with ketchup and mustard.*

Main Dishes

Pan-Roasted Chicken & Vegetables

Our Stoneware Bar Pan has ample space for roasting chicken breasts, potatoes and veggies, all at the same time. It's a complete meal in one.

2	large baking potatoes (1 pound), unpeeled
1	medium zucchini
1	medium yellow summer squash
1	large red bell pepper
1	medium red onion
4	tablespoons olive oil, divided
2	garlic cloves, pressed
1	teaspoon dried rosemary, crushed, divided
1/2	teaspoon plus 1/8 teaspoon salt, divided
1/8	teaspoon ground black pepper
1/2	cup seasoned dry bread crumbs
1	egg, lightly beaten
4	boneless, skinless chicken breast halves (about 1 1/4 pounds)

Preheat oven to 425°F. Cut potatoes, zucchini and summer squash in half lengthwise using **Garnisher**; cut potatoes crosswise into 1/4-inch slices. Cut zucchini and summer squash crosswise into 1-inch pieces. Cut bell pepper into 1-inch pieces and onion into thin wedges using **5" Utility Knife**. Place vegetables in **Stoneware Bar Pan**; toss with 2 tablespoons of the olive oil. Press garlic over vegetables using **Garlic Press**. Sprinkle with 1/2 teaspoon of the rosemary, 1/2 teaspoon of the salt and black pepper; toss to mix well. Spread vegetables around sides of pan leaving center open. Combine bread crumbs and remaining 1/2 teaspoon rosemary and 1/8 teaspoon salt in shallow bowl. Add remaining 2 tablespoons olive oil; mix well. Dip chicken in egg; coat lightly with crumb mixture. Place chicken in center of pan. Bake 22-25 minutes or until chicken is no longer pink in center.

Yield: 4 servings

Nutrients per serving: Calories 590, Fat 21 g, Sodium 970 mg, Dietary Fiber 5 g

TOOL TIP

- *To crush dried rosemary, place rosemary in small deep bowl and crush with **Mini-Tart Shaper**, applying pressure while rolling the round end of the Shaper over the leaves.*

Chicago-Style Deep-Dish Pizza

Chicagoans are proud of their deep-dish pizzas, though they never agree as to which restaurant serves the best. Maybe we should have them taste this one.

Filling

4	ounces fresh mushrooms, sliced
1/2	cup onion, chopped
1	garlic clove, pressed
1	teaspoon dried oregano leaves
1	package (10 ounces) frozen chopped spinach, thawed and well drained
1 1/2	cups pizza sauce, divided
1	can (14 1/2 ounces) Italian-seasoned diced tomatoes, drained
2	cups (8 ounces) shredded mozzarella cheese, divided
1	ounce fresh Parmesan cheese, grated (about 1/4 cup)

Crust

1/3	cup plus 1 tablespoon cornmeal, divided
1 1/2	cups all-purpose flour
1	package (1/4 ounce) quick-rising dry yeast
1	tablespoon sugar
1/2	teaspoon salt
2/3	cup very warm water (125°-130°F)
1/4	cup olive oil

Preheat oven to 425°F. For filling, slice mushrooms using **Egg Slicer Plus®**. Chop onion with **Food Chopper**. Spray **Generation II 10" Frying Pan** with olive oil. Cook mushrooms, onion, garlic and oregano over medium heat until onion is tender; stir in spinach and 1/2 cup of the pizza sauce. Remove pan from heat. In **1-Qt. Batter Bowl**, mix remaining 1 cup pizza sauce with drained tomatoes; set aside.

Lightly spray bottom of **Deep Dish Baker** with olive oil using **Kitchen Spritzer**; sprinkle with 1 tablespoon of the cornmeal. For crust, in **Classic 2-Qt. Batter Bowl**, combine flour, remaining 1/3 cup cornmeal, yeast, sugar and salt. Add water and 1/4 cup oil; stir until mixture forms a ball. Place dough on lightly floured surface; knead until smooth and elastic, about 3 minutes. Place dough in center of Baker. Using **Dough and Pizza Roller**, roll dough evenly over bottom; press up sides to edge of Baker. Sprinkle 1 cup of the mozzarella cheese over crust; top with spinach mixture, remaining 1 cup mozzarella cheese and tomato mixture. Bake 30 minutes or until crust is deep golden brown. Using **Deluxe Cheese Grater**, grate Parmesan cheese over hot pizza. Cut into wedges and serve using **Slice 'N Serve®**.

Yield: 6 servings

Nutrients per serving: Calories 410, Fat 19 g, Sodium 1190 mg, Dietary Fiber 5 g

VARIATION: Italian Sausage Deep-Dish Pizza: Reduce pizza sauce to 1 cup and mix with drained tomatoes. Substitute 8 ounces Italian sausage for the spinach. Cook sausage, mushrooms, onion, garlic and oregano until sausage is no longer pink; drain. Prepare dough, assemble pizza and bake as directed.

Double Duty Meatballs

One recipe of zesty meatballs makes two great meals.

1   jar (26-28 ounces) spaghetti sauce, divided
1/3   cup onion, chopped
1 1/2   pounds lean (90%) ground beef
3/4   cup quick or old-fashioned oats
1   egg
2   garlic cloves, pressed
1 1/2   teaspoons Italian seasoning
1/2   teaspoon salt

Preheat oven to 400°F. Spread 2/3 cup of the spaghetti sauce over bottom of **9" x 13" Baker**. Chop onion using **Food Chopper**. In **Classic 2-Qt. Batter Bowl**, combine onion, ground beef, oats, 1/3 cup of the sauce, egg, garlic, Italian seasoning and salt; mix gently. Using small **Stainless Steel Scoop**, shape meat mixture into balls; place in Baker. Bake 10 minutes. Pour remaining sauce over meatballs. Continue baking 20 minutes. Place 24 meatballs and half of the sauce from Baker in covered container; refrigerate for later use in *Spaghetti with Meatballs*. Use remaining 24 meatballs with sauce to make *Italian Meatball Sub*. Yield: 48 meatballs

Italian Meatball Sub

1/2   recipe Double Duty Meatballs (see above)
2   packages (11 ounces each) refrigerated French bread dough
    Vegetable oil
2   garlic cloves, pressed
2   tablespoons grated fresh Parmesan cheese
1   package (8 ounces) mozzarella cheese slices

Preheat oven to 350°F. Place dough, seams side down, on **15" Round Baking Stone**. Join ends of dough together to form 1 large ring. Using **Serrated Bread Knife**, cut 8 diagonal slashes (1/2 inch deep) on top of dough. Lightly spray dough with oil using **Kitchen Spritzer**. Press garlic over dough using **Garlic Press**; spread evenly. Sprinkle with Parmesan cheese. Bake 26-30 minutes or until deep golden brown. Immediately remove bread to **Nonstick Cooling Rack**; cool completely. To assemble sandwich, cut bread in half horizontally with Bread Knife. Spoon meatballs with sauce over bottom half of bread. Top with cheese slices and top half of bread. Cut into wedges and serve using **Slice 'N Serve®**. Yield: 6 servings

Nutrients per serving: Calories 540, Fat 17 g, Sodium 1420 mg, Dietary Fiber 4 g

Spaghetti with Meatballs

    Reserved 1/2 recipe Double Duty Meatballs (see above)
1   jar (14 ounces) spaghetti sauce
8   ounces uncooked spaghetti, cooked and drained

Combine reserved meatballs and sauce in **Generation II 3-Qt. Saucepan**. Cook over medium heat until meatballs are hot, stirring occasionally. Serve over hot cooked pasta. Yield: 4 servings

Nutrients per serving: Calories 400, Fat 17 g, Sodium 1250 mg, Dietary Fiber 6 g

Lasagna Primavera

Pictured on p. 2

This incredible meatless lasagna features garden fresh vegetables, Alfredo sauce and three kinds of cheese. The noodles are no fuss—they aren't cooked ahead of time.

2   cups carrots, thinly sliced
2   cups small zucchini, sliced
8   ounces mushrooms, sliced
2   tablespoons olive oil
3   garlic cloves, pressed
3/4 teaspoon dried thyme leaves
1/4 teaspoon ground black pepper
1   can (14 1/2 ounces) Italian-seasoned diced tomatoes
1   container (15 ounces) part-skim ricotta cheese
1   egg
1   ounce fresh Parmesan cheese, grated (about 1/4 cup)
1   jar (16 ounces) white Alfredo pasta sauce
3/4 cup milk
10 uncooked lasagna noodles (about 8 ounces)
3   cups (12 ounces) shredded mozzarella cheese

Preheat oven to 350°F. Thinly slice carrots using **Garnisher**. Slice zucchini using v-shaped blade of **Ultimate Slice & Grate**. Slice mushrooms using **Egg Slicer Plus®**. Heat oil in **Generation II 12" Family Skillet** over medium heat. Press garlic into oil using **Garlic Press**. Add carrots, zucchini, mushrooms, thyme and black pepper; cook, stirring occasionally, until vegetables are crisp-tender, about 7 minutes. Remove skillet from heat. Drain tomatoes and add to vegetables; set aside. In **Classic 2-Qt. Batter Bowl**, combine ricotta cheese and egg. Using **Deluxe Cheese Grater**, grate Parmesan cheese into Batter Bowl; mix well and set aside. In **1-Qt. Batter Bowl**, mix Alfredo sauce and milk.

To assemble lasagna, spread 3/4 cup of Alfredo sauce mixture over bottom of **9" x 13" Baker**. Top with half of uncooked noodles in single layer (place 4 noodles lengthwise and 1 noodle crosswise, breaking noodles to fit). Press noodles into sauce. Spread half of ricotta mixture over noodles. Top with half of vegetable mixture. Sprinkle with half of mozzarella cheese. Repeat layers, starting with 3/4 cup sauce. After layering, pour remaining sauce over top of lasagna. Cover Baker with **Rectangular Lid/Bowl**. Bake 50 minutes. Carefully remove Lid/Bowl, lifting away from you. Continue baking 10 minutes. Remove from oven; let stand 15 minutes. Cut into squares; serve using **Large Serving Spatula**.

Yield: 10 servings

Nutrients per serving: Calories 360, Fat 23 g, Sodium 1030 mg, Dietary Fiber 2 g

VARIATION: Traditional Tomato-Vegetable Lasagna: Substitute 1 jar (26-28 ounces) spaghetti sauce for Alfredo sauce. When draining tomatoes, add juice to spaghetti sauce. Omit milk. Prepare vegetable and ricotta mixtures as directed. To assemble, spread 1 cup sauce in Baker. Top with half each of noodles, ricotta mixture, vegetables and mozzarella. Top with 1 cup sauce and remaining noodles, ricotta mixture and vegetables. Spread with remaining sauce; top with remaining mozzarella. Bake as directed.

Enchiladas Extraordinaire

A flavorful chicken filling is layered between corn tortillas in our quick and easy casserole version of a Mexican favorite.

2 tablespoons fresh cilantro, snipped
4 cups shredded cooked chicken or turkey
1 can (10¾ ounces) condensed cream of chicken soup
1 package (8 ounces) shredded Mexican-style cheese blend, divided
1 cup sour cream
1 can (4 ounces) chopped green chilies, undrained
1⅛ teaspoons chili powder, divided
½ teaspoon ground cumin
11 (6-inch) corn tortillas
Vegetable oil

Preheat oven to 350°F. Snip cilantro with **Kitchen Shears**. In **Classic 2-Qt. Batter Bowl**, combine cilantro, chicken, soup, 1½ cups of the cheese, sour cream, chilies, 1 teaspoon of the chili powder and cumin; mix well. Place 4 tortillas on bottom of **9" Square Baker**, overlapping in middle. Spoon 2 cups of the chicken mixture over tortillas; spread evenly in Baker. Repeat for second layer. Top with remaining ½ cup cheese. Stack remaining 3 tortillas and cut into 16 thin triangles using **Pizza Cutter**. Sprinkle over casserole. Spray tortilla triangles with vegetable oil using **Kitchen Spritzer**. Sprinkle with remaining ⅛ teaspoon chili powder. Bake 30-35 minutes or until thoroughly heated.

Yield: 8 servings

Nutrients per serving: Calories 410, Fat 23 g, Sodium 640 mg, Dietary Fiber less than 1 g

COOK'S TIP

■ *Cilantro, also called Chinese parsley or coriander, is a fresh herb with bright green leaves and a lively, pungent fragrance. Sold in bunches, it adds a distinctive flavor to Mexican and Asian foods. To store cilantro, place bunch with stem ends down in a glass filled with enough water to cover 1 inch of the stems. Cover loosely with a plastic bag and refrigerate for up to 5 days.*

TOOL TIPS

■ *For a quick way to snip fresh cilantro, parsley and other herbs without a mess, place the herb in a small bowl and snip with the* **Kitchen Shears**.

■ *Use the* **Hold 'N Slice** *to easily shred chicken. The strong, stainless steel prongs will separate cooked chicken meat into thin long strands.*

Main Dishes

Jumpin' Jambalaya

Lively flavors abound in this traditional creole dish. The ingredient list is long, but the oven-baked preparation couldn't be easier.

1/2	cup green bell pepper, coarsely chopped
1/2	cup celery, coarsely chopped
1/4	cup onion, coarsely chopped
2	garlic cloves, pressed
1	can (14 1/2 ounces) Italian-seasoned diced tomatoes, undrained
1	cup sliced kielbasa sausage or cubed ham
1	cup uncooked converted long-grain white rice
1/2	teaspoon dried oregano leaves
1/2	teaspoon paprika
1/2	teaspoon dried thyme leaves
1/4	teaspoon salt
1/8-1/4	teaspoon ground red pepper
1	can (14 1/2 ounces) chicken broth
8	ounces uncooked, medium fresh shrimp, peeled and deveined
1/2	cup frozen peas

Preheat oven to 400°F. With **Food Chopper**, coarsely chop bell pepper, celery and onion; place in **Mini-Baking Bowl**. Press garlic into Baking Bowl using **Garlic Press**. Add tomatoes, sausage, rice and seasonings; stir. Pour broth over rice mixture; cover with **8" Mini-Baker**. Bake 55-60 minutes or until rice is tender and liquid has been absorbed. Carefully remove Baker from Bowl. Stir in shrimp and peas; cover. Let stand 10 minutes to cook shrimp until they turn pink.

Yield: 4 servings

Nutrients per serving: Calories 340, Fat 5 g, Sodium 1690 mg, Dietary Fiber 2 g

COOK'S TIPS

- *Substitute 1/2 pound boneless, skinless chicken breasts, cut into 1-inch cubes, for shrimp. Combine chicken with rice mixture before baking.*

- ***The Pampered Chef Pantry*™ *Cajun Seasoning Mix** can be substituted for the oregano, paprika, thyme, salt and ground red pepper. Use 1 tablespoon seasoning mix.*

- *Recipe ingredients can be doubled and placed in the **Stoneware Baking Bowl**. Cover with **Deep Dish Baker** and bake as directed. Yield: 8 servings*

Asian Pork Ribs

Our Rectangular Lid/Bowl does double duty here -- first as a cover to keep ribs tender and moist, then as a baking dish deep enough to hold ribs and lots of tangy sauce.

4-4¹/₂	pounds pork country-style ribs
³/₄	cup apricot or peach preserves
³/₄	cup barbecue sauce
¹/₄	cup light soy sauce
3	garlic cloves, pressed
2	teaspoons peeled fresh ginger root, finely chopped or ³/₄ teaspoon ground ginger
1	tablespoon thinly sliced green onion with tops
2	teaspoons sesame seeds

Preheat oven to 350°F. Trim excess fat from ribs. Place ribs, bone side down, in **9" x 13" Baker**. Cover with **Rectangular Lid/Bowl**. Bake 1 hour. Meanwhile, mix preserves, barbecue sauce and soy sauce in **1-Qt. Batter Bowl** with **10" Whisk**. Press garlic into bowl using **Garlic Press**. Finely chop ginger root using **Food Chopper**; add to sauce mixture. Carefully remove Rectangular Lid/Bowl from Baker. Using **Nylon Tongs**, remove ribs from Baker and place in Lid/Bowl. Generously brush ribs with half of the sauce mixture using **Pastry Brush**. Continue baking, uncovered, 30-45 minutes or until fork-tender, brushing with remaining sauce after 15 minutes. Remove ribs to serving platter. Using **Magic Mop™** skim fat from top of sauce. Sprinkle ribs with green onion and sesame seeds; serve with sauce.

Yield: 6 servings

Nutrients per serving: Calories 850, Fat 42 g, Sodium 800 mg, Dietary Fiber less than 1 g

COOK'S TIP

■ *Country-style ribs are the meatiest type of pork ribs. At the meat counter, you'll also notice they're the most economically priced.*

Turkey 'N Swiss Calzones

*Bake these turnover-style sandwiches on our Rectangle Baking Stone
for a hearty lunch or light supper.*

1	medium onion, thinly sliced
1	medium red bell pepper, thinly sliced
4	ounces mushrooms, sliced
	Olive oil
1	package (10 ounces) refrigerated pizza crust
6	ounces thinly sliced deli turkey or ham
4	teaspoons honey Dijon mustard
2	ounces thinly sliced Swiss cheese
2	garlic cloves, pressed
1/2	teaspoon dried rosemary, crushed
1/2	ounce fresh Parmesan cheese, grated (2 tablespoons)

Preheat oven to 425°F. Thinly slice onion and bell pepper with **Ultimate Slice & Grate**. Using **Egg Slicer Plus®**, slice mushrooms. Lightly spray **Generation II 10" Frying Pan** with olive oil using **Kitchen Spritzer**. Cook onion, bell pepper and mushrooms over medium heat 4-5 minutes or until tender. Unroll pizza crust dough onto **18" x 12" Grooved Cutting Board**; roll into a 12 x 10-inch rectangle using lightly floured **Dough and Pizza Roller**. With **Pizza Cutter**, cut dough in half lengthwise and crosswise to form 4 rectangles. For each calzone, place 1/4 of the turkey slices (folded to fit) on one half of one rectangle leaving 1/4-inch border. Spread turkey with 1 teaspoon mustard; top with 1/4 of the cooked vegetables and Swiss cheese. Fold other side of rectangle over filling; press edges with fork to seal. Place calzones on **12" x 15" Rectangle Baking Stone**; lightly spray tops with oil. Using **Garlic Press**, press garlic over calzones, spreading evenly. Sprinkle with rosemary. Using **Deluxe Cheese Grater**, grate Parmesan cheese over tops. Bake 14-16 minutes or until deep golden brown.

Yield: 4 calzones

Nutrients per serving (1 calzone): Calories 320 g, Fat 9 g, Sodium 980 mg, Dietary Fiber 0 g

COOK'S TIP

- *Ingredients can be doubled to make 8 sandwiches on **12" x 15" Rectangle Baking Stone**.*

TOOL TIP

- *To crush dried rosemary leaves, place rosemary in small deep bowl and crush with **Mini-Tart Shaper**, applying pressure while rolling the round end of the Shaper over the leaves.*

BBQ Chicken Twister

Pictured on p. 2

A sassy casserole of chicken, vegetables and your favorite barbecue sauce gets a fancy topper with refrigerated cornbread twists.

3	cups cooked chicken, chopped
3/4	cup celery, sliced
1	cup onion, chopped
3/4	cup green bell pepper, chopped
1	tablespoon butter or margarine
1	garlic clove, pressed
1 1/4	cups barbecue sauce
1/4	teaspoon salt
1/8	teaspoon ground black pepper
2	tablespoons cornmeal, divided (optional)
1	package (11.5 ounces) refrigerated cornbread twists

Preheat oven to 375°F. Chop chicken into bite-size pieces and slice celery using **8" Chef's Knife**. Chop onion and bell pepper using **Food Chopper**. Melt butter in **Generation II 12" Family Skillet** over medium heat. Add celery, onion, bell pepper and garlic pressed with **Garlic Press** to skillet. Cook and stir 3-4 minutes or until vegetables are tender. Add chicken, barbecue sauce, salt and black pepper. Cook 5 minutes or until mixture comes to a boil, stirring occasionally. Spoon chicken mixture into **Deep Dish Baker**. Sprinkle 1 tablespoon of the cornmeal over **18" x 12" Grooved Cutting Board**. Unroll cornbread twists over cornmeal. Sprinkle with remaining cornmeal. Separate dough into strips using **Pizza Cutter** to cut along perforations. Starting at center of Baker, twist and place half of strips over chicken mixture in spoke-like fashion. Pinch ends of strips together at center. Twist and place remaining strips around edge of Baker. Bake 20-25 minutes or until hot and bubbly.

Yield: 6 servings

Nutrients per serving: Calories 400, Fat 16 g, Sodium 1030 mg, Dietary Fiber 2 g

COOK'S TIPS

- *One package (11 ounces) refrigerated bread sticks can be substituted for cornbread twists. Starting at center of **Deep Dish Baker**, twist and place 6 bread sticks over chicken mixture in spoke-like fashion. Pinch ends together at center. Twist and place 6 bread sticks around edge of Baker.*

- *One 3-3 1/2 pound broiler-fryer chicken, cooked, will yield about 3 cups of chopped cooked chicken.*

Main Dishes

Hearty Oven Chili

*When the weather turns chilly, serve steaming bowls of chili for casual gatherings
with friends. Your homemade tortilla shells hold the toppers.*

3	pounds boneless beef chuck pot roast (arm, blade, chuck eye or shoulder) or 2½ pounds boneless beef stew meat
4	garlic cloves, pressed
2	tablespoons chili powder
1½	teaspoons dried oregano leaves
¾	teaspoon ground cumin
¾	teaspoon salt
¼	teaspoon ground black pepper
2	cups onions, coarsely chopped
2	cups green bell pepper, coarsely chopped
3	cans (14½ ounces each) diced tomatoes, undrained
2	cans (8 ounces each) tomato sauce
1	can (15.5 ounces) kidney, pinto or black beans, drained and rinsed

Tortilla Shells for toppings (optional)
Toppings such as shredded cheddar cheese, sliced ripe olives, sliced green onions and sour cream (optional)

Preheat oven to 350°F. Trim excess fat from meat with **8" Chef's Knife**. Cut meat into ½-inch cubes. Place in **Stoneware Baking Bowl**. Press garlic over meat using **Garlic Press**. Sprinkle with seasonings; stir to coat meat. Chop onions and bell pepper using **Food Chopper**. Add to Baking Bowl along with tomatoes, tomato sauce and beans. Cover Bowl with **Deep Dish Baker**. Bake 2½ hours or until meat is tender. Carefully remove Deep Dish Baker from Baking Bowl, lifting away from you. Using **Magic Mop™**, skim any fat from top of chili. Fill *Tortilla Shells* (below) with desired toppings and serve with chili.

Yield: 12 servings

Nutrients per serving (1 cup): Calories 340, Fat 10 g, Sodium 570 mg, Dietary Fiber 6 g

Tortilla Shells

3-4	(10-inch) flour tortillas

Preheat oven to 400°F. Lightly spray bottom and side of **Mini-Baking Bowl** with vegetable oil using **Kitchen Spritzer**. Gently press one tortilla onto bottom of Bowl to form a shell. (Use fingers to evenly ruffle edge of tortilla to fit inside of Bowl.) Bake 9-11 minutes or until edges are lightly browned. Remove Bowl to **Nonstick Cooling Rack**. Let tortilla cool in Bowl 5 minutes. Remove tortilla shell to Cooling Rack. Let Bowl cool 5 minutes. Place second tortilla in Bowl. Repeat baking and cooling to form remaining shells. Fill baked shells with toppings.

Thai Salmon Fillets with Cucumber Salsa

A crunchy cucumber salsa, with just a bit of heat from a jalapeño pepper, is a fresh and spirited contrast to the mildly seasoned baked salmon.

Salmon & Marinade

1	tablespoon peeled fresh ginger root, finely chopped
2	tablespoons sesame oil
1	tablespoon snipped fresh cilantro
1/4	teaspoon salt
1/4	teaspoon ground black pepper
1 1/2	pounds salmon fillets

Salsa

1	cup cucumber, chopped
1/4	cup red bell pepper, chopped
1/4	cup red onion, chopped
1	jalapeño pepper, seeded and finely chopped
1	garlic clove, pressed
3	tablespoons rice vinegar
2	tablespoons vegetable oil
1/4	teaspoon sugar
1/8	teaspoon salt

For salmon and marinade, finely chop ginger root using **Food Chopper**. Combine ginger root, sesame oil, cilantro, salt and black pepper in **1-Qt. Batter Bowl**; mix well. Place salmon fillets in resealable plastic bag; add marinade and refrigerate for at least 30 minutes or up to 6 hours. For salsa, using Food Chopper, chop cucumber, bell pepper, onion and jalapeño pepper. Using **Kitchen Scraper**, place vegetables in **Classic 2-Qt. Batter Bowl**. Press garlic into Batter Bowl using **Garlic Press**. Add vinegar, oil, sugar and salt; mix well. Preheat oven to 400°F. Remove fillets from plastic bag and place in **9" x 13" Baker**; discard marinade. Bake 15-20 minutes or until salmon turns opaque and flakes easily with a fork. Serve with salsa.

Yield: 4 servings

Nutrients per serving: Calories 340, Fat 20 g, Sodium 320 mg, Dietary Fiber less than 1 g

COOK'S TIPS

- Rice vinegar is a mild vinegar made from fermented rice. It can be found in most ethnic food sections of large supermarkets or in specialty Asian food stores. If unavailable, substitute cider vinegar in the salsa.

- Cod, halibut or haddock fillets may be substituted for the salmon fillets.

TOOL TIP

- To snip fresh cilantro, place in small, deep bowl and cut with **Kitchen Shears**.

"Fried" Chicken Salad

Refrigerated bread dough forms an edible bowl for this main dish salad.
The dough is easiest to handle when cold so keep it refrigerated until you're ready
to use it and work quickly when shaping the bread bowl.

1   package (1 ounce) dry ranch
       salad dressing & recipe mix,
       divided
1   cup milk
1   cup mayonnaise
1   package (11 ounces) refrigerated
       French bread dough
1   package (9 ounces) frozen
       breaded chicken breast fillets
       or chunks
1   package (16 ounces) iceberg
       lettuce salad mix
1   medium cucumber
1   medium green bell pepper
5   radishes, sliced
1/4 cup thinly sliced green onions with
       tops

Preheat oven to 350°F. Remove 1 teaspoon of the dressing mix to small bowl; set aside. Add remaining dressing mix and milk to **Measure, Mix, & Pour™**; mix well. Add mayonnaise; mix and refrigerate. Generously spray outside of **Stoneware Baking Bowl** with nonstick cooking spray. Place upside down on counter. Unroll bread dough onto flat side of **18" x 12" Grooved Cutting Board**. Spray lightly with nonstick cooking spray. Sprinkle evenly with reserved dry dressing mix; pat lightly onto dough. Starting on one long side, gather up dough and quickly place over outside of Baking Bowl with plain side of dough next to Bowl. Do not press dough onto Baking Bowl. Lightly pinch sides of dough together and trim off excess dough at corners with **Kitchen Shears**. Bake 15-18 minutes or until deep golden brown. Remove from oven to **Nonstick Cooling Rack**. Gently insert **Citrus Peeler** between bread and Baking Bowl to loosen. Cool bread bowl on Baking Bowl 15 minutes. Carefully remove bread from Baking Bowl. Turn upright; cool 5 minutes.

Increase oven temperature to 425°F. Place chicken on flat **Baking Stone**. Bake according to package directions until thoroughly heated. Place lettuce in bread bowl. Score cucumber using **Lemon Zester/Scorer**. Cut bell pepper into rings and thinly slice cucumber using **Ultimate Slice & Grate**. Toss vegetables with lettuce using **3-Way Tongs**. Slice chicken diagonally into thin strips. Arrange over lettuce mixture. Serve salad with dressing, tearing off pieces of bread to accompany it. Refrigerate remaining dressing for another use.

Yield: 4 servings

Nutrients per serving (2¼ cups salad, 3 tablespoons dressing and ¼ bread): Calories 530, Fat 25 g, Sodium 1140 mg, Dietary Fiber 4 g

Dazzling Desserts

Everyone saves room for dessert when the menu features recipes from The Pampered Chef. Decadent cakes, irresistible dessert squares and scrumptious cookies are just some of the sweet surprises in this delectable collection. Our Stoneware Fluted Pan gives cakes a pretty shape while our Bar Pan lets you serve sweets to a crowd with the greatest of ease. The finale is always grand when you bake with our Stoneware Collection.

Cool Lime Colada Cake

Treat your friends to a taste of the tropics.

1　package (18.25 ounces) yellow cake mix (plus ingredients to make cake)
2　limes
1　package (8 ounces) cream cheese, softened
1　cup cold milk
1　package (3.4 ounces) coconut cream or vanilla instant pudding and pie filling
1　cup thawed frozen whipped topping
3　cups assorted fresh fruit such as sliced kiwi, pineapple, apricots, nectarines, peaches, mango or papaya
2　tablespoons toasted flaked coconut (optional)

Preheat oven to 350°F. Spray **Deep Dish Baker** with nonstick cooking spray. Prepare cake mix according to package directions; pour batter into Baker. Bake 40-45 minutes or until **Cake Tester** inserted in center comes out clean. Cool on **Nonstick Cooling Rack** 10 minutes. Remove from Baker; cool completely. Cut cooled cake in half horizontally using **Serrated Bread Knife**. Place bottom half of cake on serving plate. Zest limes with **Lemon Zester/Scorer** to measure 2 teaspoons zest. Juice limes using **Lemon Aid** to measure 1/4 cup juice. Beat cream cheese in **Classic 2-Qt. Batter Bowl** with **10" Whisk** until smooth. Gradually beat in milk, a small amount at a time, until well blended. Add pudding mix; beat 1 minute. Whisk in zest and juice. Fold in whipped topping. Spread half of the pudding mixture evenly over bottom cake layer using **Large Spreader**. Top with remaining cake layer and pudding mixture. Slice peeled kiwi with **Egg Slicer Plus®**; slice remaining fruit with **5" Utility Knife**. Arrange fresh fruit over top of cake. Sprinkle with coconut, if desired.

Yield: 12 servings

Nutrients per serving: Calories 340, Fat 17 g, Sodium 440 mg, Dietary Fiber less than 1 g

COOK'S TIP

■ *To toast coconut, place coconut in **8" Mini-Baker**. Bake at 350°F for 8-10 minutes or until golden brown, stirring once.*

Fruit-Topped Triple Chocolate Pizza

Pictured on p. 2

Refrigerated chocolate chip cookie dough makes a convenient crust for this dessert pizza featuring white chocolate filling, strawberry and orange toppers and a lacy chocolate drizzle.

1   package (18 ounces) refrigerated chocolate chip cookie dough
2   squares (1 ounce each) white chocolate for baking
2   tablespoons milk
1   package (8 ounces) cream cheese, softened
1/4 cup powdered sugar
1   cup thawed frozen whipped topping
1   pint strawberries, cut in half
1   can (11 ounces) mandarin orange segments, well drained
1/4 cup semi-sweet chocolate morsels
1   tablespoon butter or margarine

Preheat oven to 350°F. For crust, shape cookie dough into a ball in center of **15" Round Baking Stone**. Using lightly floured **Dough and Pizza Roller**, roll out dough to 12-inch circle, about 1/4 inch thick. Bake 11-14 minutes or until edges are set. (Cookie will be soft. Do not overbake.) Cool 10 minutes. Carefully loosen cookie from Baking Stone using **Serrated Bread Knife**; cool completely on Baking Stone.

Microwave white chocolate and milk in **Covered Micro-Cooker®** on HIGH 1 minute; stir until smooth. Microwave an additional 10-20 seconds if necessary. Cool slightly. In **Classic 2-Qt. Batter Bowl**, combine cream cheese and powdered sugar; mix well. Gradually stir in white chocolate mixture until smooth. Fold in whipped topping; spread over crust. Arrange strawberries and mandarin oranges over cream cheese mixture. Microwave chocolate morsels and butter on HIGH 30 seconds; stir until smooth. Drizzle over fruit. Chill 30 minutes. Cut into wedges using **Slice 'N Serve®**.

Yield: 16 servings

Nutrients per serving: Calories 270, Fat 16 g, Sodium 150 mg, Dietary Fiber 1 g

TOOL TIP

- *It's important to use a **15" Round Baking Stone** for this recipe as the cookie dough crust spreads during baking.*

Peach Raspberry Crumble

Old-fashioned fruit desserts as delicious as this never go out of style.

Crumble Topping

3/4	cup all-purpose flour
1/4	cup granulated sugar
1/4	cup packed brown sugar
3/4	teaspoon ground cinnamon
1/4	cup walnuts or pecans, chopped
6	tablespoons butter or margarine, melted

Filling

1/4	cup granulated sugar
2	teaspoons cornstarch
7	cups sliced, peeled fresh peaches (about 9 medium or 3 pounds)
1/2	pint fresh raspberries (1 cup)
	Vanilla ice cream or whipped topping (optional)

Preheat oven to 375°F. For crumble topping, combine flour, sugars and cinnamon in **Classic 2-Qt. Batter Bowl**. Chop walnuts using **Food Chopper**; add to Batter Bowl. Place butter in **Covered Micro-Cooker®**. Microwave on HIGH 30-45 seconds or until melted. Add butter to ingredients in Batter Bowl; mix until crumbly and set aside. For filling, mix sugar and cornstarch; set aside. Slice peaches into 1/2-inch slices using **3" Paring Knife**. Toss peaches with cornstarch mixture in **4-Qt. Bowl** until evenly coated. Gently stir in raspberries. Spoon fruit mixture into **Deep Dish Baker**; sprinkle evenly with crumble topping. Bake 25-30 minutes or until peaches are tender and topping is golden brown. Serve warm with ice cream or whipped topping, if desired.

Yield: 8 servings

Nutrients per serving: Calories 270, Fat 11 g, Sodium 90 mg, Dietary Fiber 4 g

 COOK'S TIPS

- To peel fresh peaches, bring water to boil in **Generation II 4-Qt. Casserole**. Carefully add peaches using **Nylon Slotted Server**. Remove peaches after 1 minute and plunge into a bowl of cold water. Pull off skins using **3" Paring Knife**.

- **The Pampered Chef Pantry™ Korintje Cinnamon** can be substituted for ground cinnamon.

Tempting Toffee Crisps

These easy-to-make sweet treats are a cross between a cookie and a candy.
Be sure to use butter for the best flavor and texture.

12   whole (5 x 2½-inch) graham
      crackers
¾   cup packed brown sugar
¾   cup butter (do not use margarine)
1   teaspoon vanilla
1   cup semi-sweet chocolate morsels
½   cup almonds, chopped

Preheat oven to 350°F. Arrange graham crackers side by side in single layer in **Stoneware Bar Pan**. In **Generation II 2-Qt. Saucepan**, combine brown sugar, butter and vanilla. Cook over medium heat, stirring occasionally with **Bamboo Spoon**, until mixture comes to a full boil across the surface. Continue boiling 4 minutes, stirring constantly. Remove saucepan from heat and immediately pour mixture evenly over crackers. Bake 10-12 minutes or until bubbly and lightly browned. Remove pan from oven to **Nonstick Cooling Rack**. Sprinkle with chocolate morsels; allow to soften then spread evenly over baked crackers using **Large Spreader**. Chop almonds using **Food Chopper**; sprinkle over chocolate. Cool completely. Refrigerate until chocolate is firm. Break or cut into pieces.

Yield: About 2 dozen pieces

Nutrients per serving (1 piece): Calories 150, Fat 10 g, Sodium 110 mg, Dietary Fiber less than 1 g

COOK'S TIPS

■ *Once the chocolate is firm, the crisps should be stored in a cool place at room temperature. Keep them tightly covered so the graham crackers will stay crisp.*

■ *Substitute peanuts, pecans or walnuts for almonds, or omit nuts, if desired.*

Bonanza Brownie Bars

Divide one Bar Pan of homemade brownies into three sections and choose a different topping for each. You're sure to please everyone.

Brownies

1¼	cups all-purpose flour
1¼	cups unsweetened cocoa powder
1¼	cups butter or margarine
2½	cups sugar
5	eggs
2	teaspoons vanilla

Topping

    Choose 3 Variations (see below)

Preheat oven to 325°F. Spray **Stoneware Bar Pan** with nonstick cooking spray. For brownies, combine flour and cocoa powder in **1-Qt. Batter Bowl**; set aside. Melt butter in **Generation II 3-Qt. Saucepan** over medium-low heat. Remove saucepan from heat. Stir in sugar using **Mix 'N Scraper®**. Add eggs, one at a time, mixing well after each addition. Stir in vanilla. Gradually add flour mixture, mixing until well blended. Spread evenly in pan. Bake 28-33 minutes or until edges are firm. (Do not overbake.) Cool completely in pan. For topping, cut brownies crosswise into three even sections; top each section with a Topping Variation. Cut each section into 15 bars.

Yield: 45 brownies

Nutrients per serving (1 brownie with vanilla frosting): Calories 150, Fat 7 g, Sodium 70 mg, Dietary Fiber 1 g

VARIATIONS

*For each section (⅓ pan of brownies),
spread with ½ cup prepared frosting and sprinkle with topping:*

- **Candy Topped:**
  Vanilla or chocolate frosting; 2 tablespoons miniature candy-coated chocolate pieces or jelly beans.
- **Confetti Fun:**
  Vanilla or chocolate frosting; 1 tablespoon multi-colored sprinkles or nonpareils.
- **Cookies 'N Creme:**
  Vanilla frosting; 4 creme-filled chocolate sandwich cookies, chopped.

- **German Chocolate:**
  Coconut-pecan frosting; ¼ cup chopped pecans.
- **Mocha Chip:**
  Vanilla frosting mixed with combined ½ teaspoon instant coffee granules and 1 teaspoon hot water; 2 tablespoons miniature semi-sweet chocolate morsels.
- **Nutty Chocolate:**
  Chocolate frosting; ¼ cup chopped nuts.

- **Peanut Butter 'N Chocolate:**
  Chocolate frosting blended with 2 tablespoons peanut butter; ¼ cup chopped peanuts.
- **Peppermint Stick:**
  Vanilla frosting; 2 tablespoons chopped hard peppermint candies.

Plum Delicious Spice Cake

*Use a combination of red and purple plums for the prettiest
topping to this homey dessert.*

4	medium red or purple plums
1	package (about 16 ounces) nut or date quick bread mix
1¼	teaspoons ground cinnamon, divided
¼	teaspoon ground ginger
1	cup milk
⅓	cup vegetable oil
1	egg
1	tablespoon sugar
¼	cup currant jelly, heated
	Thawed frozen whipped topping (optional)

Preheat oven to 350°F. Spray **9" Square Baker** with nonstick cooking spray. Core plums using **The Corer**. Slice into rings using v-shaped blade of **Ultimate Slice & Grate**. Cut rings in half crosswise; set aside. In **Classic 2-Qt. Batter Bowl**, combine bread mix, 1 teaspoon of the cinnamon and ginger. Add milk, oil and egg. Stir 50-75 strokes using **Mix 'N Scraper®** until well blended. Spread into Baker. Arrange plums over batter. Combine sugar and remaining ¼ teaspoon cinnamon in **Flour/Sugar Shaker**. Sprinkle over plums. Bake 45-50 minutes or until **Cake Tester** inserted in center comes out clean. Heat jelly in **Covered Micro-Cooker®** on HIGH 1 minute or until smooth when stirred. Brush over cake using **Pastry Brush**. Cool at least 30 minutes. Cut into squares. Serve warm or at room temperature using **Large Serving Spatula**. Using **Easy Accent Decorator™**, garnish each serving with whipped topping, if desired.

Yield: 9 servings

Nutrients per serving: Calories 340, Fat 14 g, Sodium 270 mg, Dietary Fiber 2 g

COOK'S TIP

- It's best to use slightly firm plums that have just started to ripen. Plums should be plump and yield slightly to gentle pressure. To ripen plums at home, store them for 1 to 2 days in a closed paper bag at room temperature.

Cranberry Macadamia Oat Cookies

Pictured on p. 2

*We've splurged on these oatmeal cookies and made them for grownups by
adding white chocolate, macadamia nuts and dried cranberries.
We bet your kids will find them irresistible, too!*

1¹/₃	cups all-purpose flour
¹/₂	teaspoon baking powder
¹/₂	teaspoon baking soda
¹/₄	teaspoon salt
1	cup butter or margarine, softened
³/₄	cup packed brown sugar
¹/₂	cup granulated sugar
2	eggs
1	teaspoon vanilla
4	squares (1 ounce each) white chocolate for baking, coarsely chopped
1	jar (3.25 ounces) macadamia nuts, coarsely chopped (³/₄ cup)
2¹/₂	cups old-fashioned or quick oats
1	cup dried cranberries

Preheat oven to 375°F. In **1-Qt. Batter Bowl**, combine flour, baking powder, baking soda and salt; mix well. In **Classic 2-Qt. Batter Bowl**, beat butter and sugars until creamy. Add eggs and vanilla; beat well. Add flour mixture; mix well. Using **Food Chopper**, coarsely chop white chocolate and nuts; transfer to Batter Bowl using **Kitchen Scraper**. Stir in oats and cranberries; mix well. Using medium **Stainless Steel Scoop**, drop 9 rounded scoops of dough, 2 inches apart, onto **12" x 15" Rectangle Baking Stone**. (Cookies will spread while baking.) Flatten balls slightly. Bake 14-16 minutes or until edges are golden brown. Cool 5 minutes on Baking Stone; remove to **Nonstick Cooling Rack**. Repeat with remaining dough. Cool completely. Store in tightly covered container.

Yield: About 3 dozen cookies

Nutrients per serving: Calories 150, Fat 9 g, Sodium 100 mg, Dietary Fiber 1 g

COOK'S TIP

- *You can substitute raisins or dried cherries, blueberries or mixed fruits for the cranberries, and almonds, pecans or walnuts for the macadamia nuts.*

Marble Cheesecake Squares

*Don't let anyone know just how easy it is to make these fancy squares.
Just enjoy the compliments.*

24	creme-filled chocolate sandwich cookies, finely chopped (about 2 cups)
3	tablespoons butter or margarine, melted
4	packages (8 ounces each) cream cheese, softened
1	cup sugar
1	teaspoon vanilla
4	eggs
1	cup sour cream
1	square (1 ounce) semi-sweet chocolate for baking (not unsweetened chocolate), melted

Preheat oven to 350°F. Chop cookies using **Food Chopper**; place in **1-Qt. Batter Bowl** using **Kitchen Scraper**. Place butter in **Covered Micro-Cooker®**. Microwave on HIGH 30 seconds or until melted. Add to Batter Bowl; mix well. Press crumb mixture onto bottom of **Stoneware Bar Pan**. In **Classic 2-Qt. Batter Bowl**, beat cream cheese, sugar and vanilla until well blended. Add eggs, one at a time, mixing well after each addition. Stir in sour cream until well blended. Remove ¾ cup batter to small bowl. Stir in melted chocolate; set aside. Pour remaining batter over crust, carefully spreading to edges of pan with **Super Scraper**. Place chocolate batter in **Easy Accent Decorator™** fitted with **Bismarck Tip**. Pipe chocolate batter in 5 lengthwise stripes equal distance apart on top of batter. Using **5" Utility Knife**, cut crosswise through batter several times for marble effect. Bake 18-20 minutes or until set. Remove pan to **Nonstick Cooling Rack**. Cool bars to room temperature. Refrigerate. Cut into squares; serve using **Mini-Serving Spatula**.

Yield: 24 squares

Nutrients per servings: Calories 270, Fat 20 g, Sodium 230 mg, Dietary Fiber 0 g

Chocolate Satin Mint Cake

*Special occasions call for show-stopping desserts. This decadent cake, filled with
a minty cream cheese ribbon, is definitely worth the effort to make.*

Filling

- 1 package (8 ounces) cream cheese, softened
- 1/4 cup sugar
- 2 tablespoons butter or margarine, softened
- 1 tablespoon cornstarch
- 1 egg
- 2 tablespoons milk
- 3/4 teaspoon peppermint extract

Cake

- 1 package (18.25 ounces) devil's food cake mix
- 1 cup water
- 1/3 cup vegetable oil
- 3 eggs

Glaze & Drizzle

- 1/3 cup light corn syrup
- 1/3 cup whipping cream
- 6 squares (1 ounce each) semi-sweet chocolate for baking (not unsweetened chocolate), finely chopped
- 2 squares (1 ounce each) white chocolate for baking
- 2 teaspoons vegetable oil
- 1/4 teaspoon peppermint extract

Preheat oven to 325°F. Spray **Stoneware Fluted Pan** with nonstick cooking spray. For filling, beat cream cheese, sugar, butter and cornstarch in **1-Qt. Batter Bowl** until well blended. Add egg, milk and extract. Mix until smooth; set aside. For cake, in **Classic 2-Qt. Batter Bowl**, combine cake mix, water, oil and eggs; mix according to package directions. Spread 2 cups cake batter evenly in pan. Spread evenly with filling. Slowly pour remaining cake batter over filling. Bake 55-65 minutes or until **Cake Tester** inserted near center comes out clean. Cool in pan 10 minutes. Loosen cake from edge and center of pan. Invert onto **Nonstick Cooling Rack**. Cool completely. Place rack over **Cutting Board** covered with **Parchment Paper**.

For glaze, in **Generation II 1½-Qt. Saucepan**, bring corn syrup and whipping cream to a simmer over medium heat, stirring constantly with **Nylon Spiral Whisk**. Remove saucepan from heat. Add semi-sweet chocolate, stirring until smooth. Spread 2/3 cup glaze smoothly over top and side of cake using **Skinny Scraper**. Freeze cake 5 minutes until glaze is almost set. Meanwhile, keep remaining glaze warm over medium-low heat. Slowly pour over cake. Remove cake to serving platter. Refrigerate until glaze is firm, about 1 hour. For drizzle, microwave white chocolate and oil in **Covered Micro-Cooker®** on HIGH 1 minute 30 seconds or until mixture is smooth when stirred. Stir in extract. Drizzle over cake. Refrigerate 15 minutes. Cut into slices using **Slice 'N Serve®.** Yield: 16 servings

Nutrients per serving: Calories 380, Fat 22 g, Sodium 340 mg, Dietary Fiber 3 g

COOK'S TIP

- *For whipped cream garnish, beat 2/3 cup whipping cream with 2 tablespoons sugar until stiff. Attach **Open Star Tip** to **Easy Accent Decorator**™; garnish cake with whipped cream rosettes, edible flowers and fresh mint.*

Desserts

Black Forest Ice Cream Cake

Our heavenly cake roll features chocolate chip ice cream in a cocoa-flavored angel food cake. Frozen and sliced, it's garnished with a drizzle of chocolate, a spoonful of cherries and a swirl of whipped topping.

1	package (16 ounces) angel food cake mix
1/4	cup unsweetened cocoa powder
1/2	cup powdered sugar
4	cups (1 quart) chocolate chip ice cream, softened
1 1/2	cups chocolate-flavored syrup
1	can (21 ounces) cherry pie filling
1 1/2	cups thawed frozen whipped topping

Preheat oven to 350°F. Cut an 18-inch long piece of **Parchment Paper**. Press into bottom and up sides of **Stoneware Bar Pan**. Add cocoa powder to angel food cake mix and mix according to package directions. Pour batter into pan; spread evenly using **Super Scraper**. Cut through batter to remove large air bubbles. Bake 30 minutes or until top springs back when lightly touched with fingertip. Remove from oven to **Nonstick Cooling Rack**. Sprinkle powdered sugar over cake using **Flour/Sugar Shaker**. Place a sheet of parchment paper over cake. Place cooling rack upside down over parchment paper and carefully turn cake out at once. Remove pan and parchment paper from cooked side of cake. Starting at one of the short sides, roll up cake in parchment paper. Cool completely on cooling rack.

Unroll cake and transfer to **18" x 12" Grooved Cutting Board**; discard parchment paper. Carefully spread cake with softened ice cream to within 1 inch of edges; re-roll cake. Sprinkle with additional powdered sugar. Wrap cake in aluminum foil; freeze until firm, at least 4 hours. When ready to serve, let wrapped cake roll stand at room temperature 10-20 minutes. Cut into 1-inch slices using **Serrated Bread Knife**. For each serving, drizzle 2 tablespoons syrup over dessert plate using **V-Shaped Cutter**; top with cake slice. Spoon about 3 tablespoons pie filling over cake. Garnish with whipped topping using **Easy Accent Decorator™**. Sprinkle with additional cocoa powder, if desired.

Yield: 12 servings

Nutrients per serving: Calories 430, Fat 9 g, Sodium 400 mg, Dietary Fiber 2 g

Pumpkin Pie à la Easy

Entertaining is easier than ever when you bake up this crowd-pleasing pumpkin dessert in our Stoneware Bar Pan.

1¼   cups all-purpose flour
¾   cup quick or old-fashioned oats
½   cup packed brown sugar
½   cup pecans, chopped
⅔   cup butter or margarine, melted
4   eggs
2   cans (15 ounces each) solid
      pack pumpkin
2   cans (14 ounces each) sweetened
      condensed milk (not
      evaporated milk)
2   teaspoons ground cinnamon
1   teaspoon ground ginger
½   teaspoon ground nutmeg
1   teaspoon salt
      Thawed frozen whipped topping
      (optional)
      Pecan halves (optional)

Preheat oven to 350°F. In **Classic 2-Qt. Batter Bowl**, combine flour, oats and brown sugar. Chop pecans using **Food Chopper**. Add to Batter Bowl. Melt butter in **Covered Micro-Cooker®** on HIGH 1 minute or until melted. Add to dry ingredients; mix well. Press mixture onto bottom of **Stoneware Bar Pan**. Bake 15 minutes. Meanwhile, lightly beat eggs in Batter Bowl using **10" Whisk**. Add pumpkin, sweetened condensed milk, spices and salt; whisk until smooth. Pour over crust. Bake 30-35 minutes or until filling is set and knife inserted in center comes out clean. Let cool at room temperature. Cut into squares; serve using **Mini-Serving Spatula**. Garnish each serving with whipped topping using **Easy Accent Decorator™** pecan halves and additional ground cinnamon, if desired. Refrigerate any leftover pie squares.

Yield: 24 servings

Nutrients per serving: Calories 230, Fat 11 g, Sodium 200 mg, Dietary Fiber 2 g

COOK'S TIP

■ *This recipe can be made in the **9" Square Baker**. Divide ingredient amounts in half and bake as directed. Yield: 12 servings*

■ *Be sure to purchase canned pumpkin, not pumpkin pie filling, for this recipe.*

■ *You can substitute 3½ teaspoons pumpkin pie spice for the ground cinnamon, ginger and nutmeg.*

Cinnamon Pecan Biscotti

These popular Italian cookies are actually baked twice! The second baking makes them crisp and crunchy. Packaged in pretty tins, they're perfect for gift-giving.

1/2 cup pecans, chopped and toasted
2 cups all-purpose flour
1 teaspoon baking powder
1 teaspoon ground cinnamon
6 tablespoons butter or margarine, softened
3/4 cup sugar
2 eggs
1 teaspoon vanilla
2 teaspoons sugar for topping

Preheat oven to 350°F. Chop pecans using **Food Chopper**. Place in **Stoneware Bar Pan**. Bake 6-7 minutes or until lightly toasted; remove from pan and cool. In **1-Qt. Batter Bowl**, combine flour, baking powder and cinnamon; set aside. In **Classic 2-Qt. Batter Bowl**, beat butter and 3/4 cup sugar until creamy. Beat in eggs and vanilla. Add flour mixture; mix well. Stir in pecans. Divide dough in half. Form each half into a 7 x 2-inch log. Lightly spray Bar Pan with nonstick cooking spray. Place each log crosswise in pan about 4 inches apart. Sprinkle each with 1 teaspoon sugar. Bake 30 minutes. Remove pan to **Nonstick Cooling Rack**; let logs cool in pan 15 minutes. Carefully remove logs to **18" x 12" Grooved Cutting Board** using **Large Serving Spatula**. With **Serrated Bread Knife**, gently cut logs diagonally into 1/2-inch-thick slices. Arrange slices upright in pan, about 1 inch apart. Bake 20-25 minutes or until dry and crisp. Cool completely on cooling rack. Store in tightly covered container.

Yield: About 2 dozen cookies

Nutrients per serving (1 cookie): Calories 110, Fat 5 g, Sodium 45 mg, Dietary Fiber 0 g

VARIATIONS: Cranberry Apricot Biscotti: Omit pecans and cinnamon. Add 1 teaspoon grated orange zest with eggs. Stir 1/4 cup each dried cranberries and finely chopped dried apricots into dough. Bake as directed. **Mocha Chip Biscotti:** Omit pecans and cinnamon. Dissolve 1 tablespoon instant coffee granules in 1 teaspoon warm water. Add with eggs. Stir 1/2 cup miniature semi-sweet chocolate morsels into dough. Omit sugar for topping. Bake as directed. To drizzle with chocolate, microwave 1/3 cup miniature semi-sweet chocolate morsels and 2 tablespoons butter or margarine in Covered Micro-Cooker® on HIGH 1 minute; stir. Continue microwaving 10-30 seconds or until mixture is smooth when stirred. Drizzle over biscotti. Refrigerate 20 minutes or until chocolate drizzle is firm.

Old-Fashioned Apple Pie Squares

*Everyone's favorite, apple pie, takes on a new shape when baked in our
Stoneware Bar Pan. With eighteen generous servings, there's plenty for seconds.*

Crust & Filling

1	package (15 ounces) refrigerated pie crusts (2 crusts)
3/4	cup granulated sugar
1 1/2	teaspoons ground cinnamon
1/2	teaspoon salt
6	medium Granny Smith apples (about 2 1/2 pounds)
1	egg, lightly beaten

Glaze

1	cup powdered sugar
5-6	teaspoons milk

Preheat oven to 400°F. For crust and filling, let pie crusts stand at room temperature 15 minutes. Combine granulated sugar, cinnamon and salt in **Flour/Sugar Shaker**; set aside. Lightly flour flat side of **18" x 12" Grooved Cutting Board**; roll one pie crust to a 16 x 11-inch rectangle using lightly floured **Dough and Pizza Roller**. Fold crust in half, then in quarters. Place crust in **Stoneware Bar Pan**; unfold and fit loosely into bottom of pan. Peel, core and slice apples using **Apple Peeler/Corer/Slicer** to make about 8 cups slices. Cut slices crosswise in half; layer apples in even rows over crust in pan. Sprinkle sugar mixture over apples. Roll remaining crust into a 16 x 11-inch rectangle; fold in half, then in quarters. Gently unfold crust over apples. (Do not seal edges.) Using **V-Shaped Cutter**, cut several slits in top crust; brush with egg using **Pastry Brush**. Bake 30-35 minutes or until apples are tender and crust is deep golden brown. For glaze, mix powdered sugar and milk until smooth; drizzle over warm pastry using V-Shaped Cutter. Cut into squares. Serve warm or at room temperature using **Mini-Serving Spatula**.

Yield: 18 squares

Nutrients per serving: Calories 190, Fat 7 g, Sodium 190 mg, Dietary Fiber 1 g

COOK'S TIPS

■ *The Pampered Chef Pantry™ **Korintje Cinnamon** can be substituted for ground cinnamon.*

■ *As pie crusts are rolled, they can be cut and patched in corners in order to better fit in the **Stoneware Bar Pan**. Folding the rolled crusts into quarters makes it easier to transfer crusts from the cutting board to the Bar Pan without stretching. Stretched crusts will shrink during baking.*

Strawberry Rhubarb Cake

The delicious fruit combo starts on top of the cake batter but magically travels to the bottom of the Baker during baking.

3   cups fresh rhubarb, cut into
      ¼-inch slices
1   pint fresh strawberries, sliced
      (2 cups)
1   package (18.25 ounces) white
      cake mix
1   cup water
⅓   cup vegetable oil
2   eggs
1   medium orange
1   cup sugar
1   cup thawed frozen whipped
      topping

Preheat oven to 350°F. Cut rhubarb in ¼-inch slices using **8" Chef's Knife**. Place in **4-Qt. Bowl**. Slice strawberries into Batter Bowl using **Egg Slicer Plus™**; mix lightly. In **Classic 2-Qt. Batter Bowl**, combine cake mix, water, oil and eggs; mix according to package directions. Zest orange with **Lemon Zester/Scorer** to measure 2 tablespoons plus 1½ teaspoons zest. Stir 2 tablespoons of the zest into cake batter; set aside remaining zest. Spread batter evenly in **9" x 13" Baker**. Top with fruit mixture. Sprinkle with sugar using **Flour/Sugar Shaker**. Bake 45-50 minutes or until **Cake Tester** inserted in center comes out clean. Fold remaining orange zest into whipped topping. Attach **Open Star Tip** to **Easy Accent Decorator™**; fill with whipped topping mixture. Cut cake into squares; serve warm using **Mini-Serving Spatula**. Garnish each serving with whipped topping mixture.

Yield: 12 servings

Nutrients per serving: Calories 350, Fat 13 g, Sodium 300 mg, Dietary Fiber 2 g

METRIC CONVERSION CHART

Volume Measurements (dry)
⅛ teaspoon = 0.5 mL
¼ teaspoon = 1 mL
½ teaspoon = 2 mL
¾ teaspoon = 4 mL
1 teaspoon = 5 mL
1 tablespoon = 15 mL
2 tablespoons = 30 mL
¼ cup = 60 mL
⅓ cup = 75 mL
½ cup = 125 mL
⅔ cup = 150 mL
¾ cup = 175 mL
1 cup = 250 mL
2 cups = 1 pint = 500 mL
3 cups = 750 mL
4 cups = 1 quart = 1 L

Volume Measurements (fluid)
1 fluid ounce (2 tablespoons) = 30 mL
4 fluid ounces (½ cup) = 125 mL
8 fluid ounces (1 cup) = 250 mL
12 fluid ounces (1½ cups) = 375 mL
16 fluid ounces (2 cups) = 500 mL

Weights (mass)
½ ounce = 15 g
1 ounce = 30 g
3 ounces = 90 g
4 ounces = 120 g
8 ounces = 225 g
10 ounces = 285 g
12 ounces = 360 g
16 ounces = 1 pound = 450 g

Dimensions
1/16 inch = 2 mm
⅛ inch = 3 mm
¼ inch = 6 mm
½ inch = 1.5 cm
¾ inch = 2 cm
1 inch = 2.5 cm

Oven Temperatures
250°F = 120°C
275°F = 140°C
300°F = 150°C
325°F = 160°C
350°F = 180°C
375°F = 190°C
400°F = 200°C
425°F = 220°C
450°F = 230°C

Getting to Know Your Stoneware

As a proud owner of one or more pieces in The Pampered Chef Family Heritage® Stoneware Collection, you can make the most of your investment by following our use and care guidelines when preparing recipes from the **More Stoneware Sensations** cookbook. Whether you are a new stoneware cook or an experienced stoneware baker, reviewing the answers to our most frequently asked stoneware questions will enhance your baking success.

Q: How is stoneware made?

A: Family Heritage® Stoneware is made from natural stoneware clay. When fired at over 2000°F temperatures, this clay produces a buff-colored stoneware that is unaffected by moisture and completely safe for use with food. After firing, each Family Heritage® piece is hand finished, producing a one-of-a-kind creation. This is why no two pieces of stoneware look or feel exactly alike.

Q: What are the benefits of baking with stoneware?

A: The benefits are numerous. Because it heats evenly and then retains that heat, stoneware produces exceptionally crisp crusts and moist interiors, promotes even baking and browning, and roasts foods to perfection.

Preparing to Use Your Stoneware

Q: What do I need to do to my stoneware before I use it for the first time?

A: First of all, do not soak stoneware in water before using. Rinse the stoneware in warm water, then towel dry and season.

Q: How should stoneware be seasoned?

A: Season stoneware by baking a high-fat food, such as refrigerated dough for dinner rolls, biscuits, or cookies, on its surface. Afterwards, greasing is usually unnecessary. If food does stick slightly, for the next few uses *lightly* spray the surface with nonstick cooking spray. Wipe off excess spray using paper towels so that the stoneware does not become sticky. Seasoning occurs when fats and oils from foods gradually adhere to the stoneware's surface. This does not pose a threat to food safety. As your stoneware becomes increasingly seasoned, it forms a nonstick coating. The color of your stoneware will also gradually change from its natural color to a deep brown. In fact, the darker its surface becomes, the better its baking qualities, much like a well-seasoned cast-iron skillet.

Baking with Stoneware

Q: How durable is stoneware?

A: Stoneware is durable, but not indestructible. The most important fact to remember about your stoneware is that it doesn't like extreme and sudden temperature changes or what is called thermal shock. When thermal shock occurs, stoneware may develop small hairline cracks or break.

Q: How do I choose the right piece of stoneware for my cooking?

A: Always use a stoneware piece that closely matches the size of the food item being prepared. To prevent your stoneware piece from breaking during baking, it's best to cover about two-thirds of the surface area with food.

Q: Should I preheat my oven before baking with stoneware?

A: Yes. However, do *not* preheat empty stoneware in the oven because this may cause the stoneware to crack or break.

Q: How do I adapt my old recipes, made in standard bakeware, so that they will work with my new stoneware?

A: Use the same baking times and temperatures with stoneware as you would with other bakeware. The only exception is if the food requires a baking time under 10 minutes. You may need to bake these items an additional 1 to 2 minutes.

Q: Can stoneware be used to cook frozen foods?

A: Thick, dense foods, such as chicken parts, fish fillets or pork chops, should be thawed completely before cooking. Putting a frozen pizza or frozen precooked foods, such as chicken nuggets, French fries and fish sticks, on stoneware is fine. Just be sure to evenly distribute small pieces over the surface.

Q: Can I freeze a casserole in a stoneware baker then transfer it directly from the freezer to the oven to bake?

A: No, do not transfer any stoneware piece directly from the freezer to the oven. Foods can be frozen in stoneware pieces but must be placed in the refrigerator to thaw completely before being baked.

Q: Can stoneware be used in the microwave?

A: Stoneware can safely be used in the microwave oven. However, foods will not become crisp or brown.

Q: Can stoneware be used when broiling foods?

A: No, stoneware cannot be used under the broiler or directly over a heat source, such as a range-top burner.

Q: How do I use stoneware in my convection oven?

A: When using stoneware in a convection oven, remember to reduce the oven temperature and baking time as specified by the oven manufacturer. If foods are browning too quickly, lightly cover the surface of the food with aluminum foil for part of the baking time.

Caring for Your Stoneware

Q: Can stoneware break?

A: Yes, but with a little tender care you can prevent your stoneware from cracking or breaking. Never immerse hot stoneware in water or pour water or other liquids into or onto it. Avoid dropping stoneware or knocking it against a hard surface.

Don't stack stoneware pieces or place other heavy utensils, such as bowls or cookware, on top of them. If you must store your stoneware on a rack in the oven, be sure to remove all the pieces before turning on the oven.

Q: Will I harm the surface of my stoneware if I cut foods on it?

A: No. Foods may be cut directly on the stoneware for serving.

Q: What is the best way to clean my stoneware?

A: The stoneware must be completely cool before cleaning. Scrape off any excess food using the Nylon Pan Scraper that came with your stoneware or The Pampered Chef Easy Clean™ Kitchen Brush. If necessary, soak the stoneware in clear, hot water to loosen baked-on foods. Rinse and dry thoroughly.

Q: Can I use soap?

A: It is important that you do not use soap or detergent when cleaning stoneware. The soap will attach itself to the fats and oils in the seasoning and remain on the surface, giving a soapy flavor to the next foods that are baked on it. Stoneware should not be washed in a dishwasher.

Q: Without soap, how can my stoneware really be clean and safe from harmful bacteria?

A: If you follow the simple cleaning instructions above, the stoneware cannot harbor any harmful bacteria that would pose a threat to food safety. Because the surface of the stoneware is nonporous, no food particles or juices can be imbedded in the stoneware. Stoneware is safe to use as long as all food particles are removed from the surface and it is dried thoroughly before storing.

By practicing these guidelines, your stoneware will last for many years. As you experience the superb baking results of stoneware, you will recognize the quality, value and high-performance that The Family Heritage® Stoneware Collection represents.

Recipe Index